CREATE GRAPHICAL USER INTERFACES WITH PYTHON

First published in 2020 by Raspberry Pi Trading Ltd, Maurice Wilkes Building,
St. John's Innovation Park, Cowley Road, Cambridge, CB4 0DS

Publishing Director: Russell Barnes • Editor: Phil King
Design: Critical Media
CEO: Eben Upton

ISBN: 978-1-912047-91-8

The publisher and contributors accept no responsibility in respect of any omissions or errors relating to goods, products or services referred to or advertised in this book. Except where otherwise noted, the content of this book is licensed under a Creative Commons Attribution-NonCommercial-ShareAlike 3.0 Unported
(CC BY-NC-SA 3.0)

About the authors...

Martin O'Hanlon

Martin works in the learning team at the Raspberry Pi Foundation, where he creates online courses, projects, and learning resources. He contributes to the development of many open-source projects and Python libraries, including guizero. As a child, he wanted to be a computer scientist, astronaut, or snowboard instructor.

Laura Sach

Laura leads the A Level team at the Raspberry Pi Foundation, creating resources for students to learn about Computer Science. She somehow also manages to make cakes, hug cats, and wrangle a toddler.

Welcome!

This book will show you how to use Python to create some fun graphical user interfaces (GUIs) using the guizero library. The guizero library started with the belief that there must be an easier way for students in school to create Python GUIs. The library itself was born one day on a long train journey from Cambridge, as the side project of a secondary school teacher.

Guizero has grown significantly in terms of features, yet remained true to its original aim of being simple but flexible. It is a library for all beginners to create with, for teachers to scaffold learning with and for experts to save time with.

We hope that these projects and guizero brings you that little spark of excitement to your Python programs. That spark might be anything from a button that does something when you click it, to colours in your otherwise black and white Python programming, to a full multicoloured Waffle.

It turns out that with open-source software, even if you don't know how to get the whole way there, if you start, someone will help you. We are grateful to the many contributors who have put time and effort into creating guizero, and to the thousands of people who have used it in their projects. Enjoy your journey and be proud of your creations.

Laura and Martin

Contents

Chapter 1: Introduction to GUIs　　　　　　　　　　　　　　**008**
How to install guizero and create your first app

Chapter 2: Wanted Poster　　　　　　　　　　　　　　　　　**012**
Use styled text and an image to create a poster

Chapter 3: Spy Name Chooser　　　　　　　　　　　　　　　**018**
Make an interactive GUI application

Chapter 4: Meme Generator　　　　　　　　　　　　　　　　**026**
Create a GUI application which draws memes

Chapter 5: World's Worst GUI　　　　　　　　　　　　　　　**036**
Learn good GUI design by doing it all wrong first!

Chapter 6: Tic-tac-toe　　　　　　　　　　　　　　　　　　**044**
Use your GUI to control a simple game

Chapter 7: Destroy the Dots　　　　　　　　　　　　　　　**062**
Learn how to use a Waffle to create a tasty game

Chapter 8: Flood It   078
Create a more complex Waffle-based puzzle game

Chapter 9: Emoji Match   092
Make a fun picture-matching game

Chapter 10: Paint   110
Create a simple drawing application

Chapter 11: Stop-frame Animation   124
Build your own stop-frame animated GIF creator

Appendix A: Setting up   138
Learn how install Python and an IDE

Appendix B: Get started with Python   142
How to start coding in Python

Appendix C: Widgets in guizero   148
An overview of the widgets used in guizero

Chapter 1
Introduction to GUIs
How to install guizero and create your first app

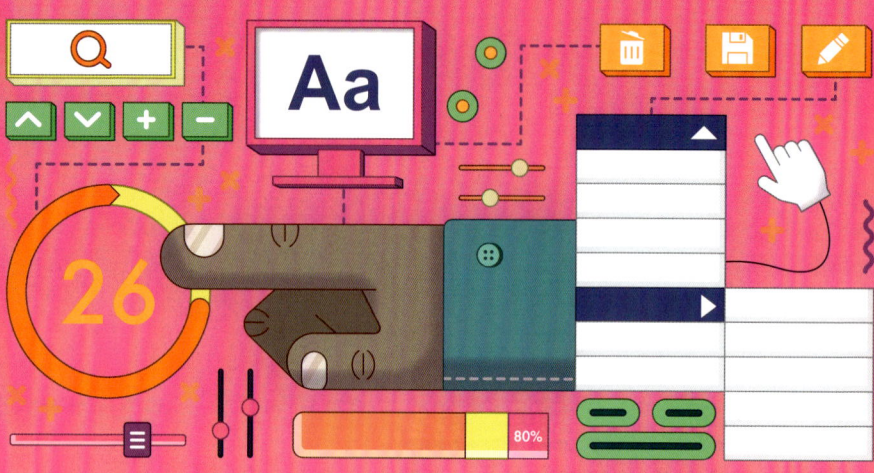

WHAT YOU'LL NEED

You will need a computer (e.g. Raspberry Pi, Apple Mac, Windows or Linux PC) and an internet connection for the software installation. You will also need the following software installed:

- **Python 3** (python.org) – see Appendix A

- **An IDE** (code editor), e.g.:
  IDLE (installed with Python 3), Thonny (thonny.org), Mu (codewith.mu), PyCharm (jetbrains.com/pycharm)

- **The guizero Python library** (lawsie.github.io/guizero)

A graphical user interface (GUI, pronounced 'gooey') is a way of making your Python programs easier to use and more exciting. You can add different components called 'widgets' to your interface, allowing lots of different ways for information to be entered in to the program and displayed as output. You might want to allow people to push a button, to display a piece of text, or even let them choose an option from a menu. In this book we will use the guizero library, which has been developed with the aim of helping beginners to easily create GUIs.

Python's standard GUI package is called tkinter, and is already installed with Python on most platforms. The guizero library is a wrapper for tkinter – this means that it offers a much simpler way of using Python's standard GUI library.

Installing guizero

You will need to install the guizero (**lawsie.github.io/guizero**) Python library to create the programs in this book. It is available as a Python package, which is reusable code you can download, install, and then use in your programs.

▲ An alternative way to install guizero is to download the zip file from GitHub

How you install of guizero will depend on your operating system and the permissions you have to control your computer.

If you have access to the command line / terminal, you can use the following command:

```
pip3 install guizero
```

Comprehensive installation instructions for guizero are available at **lawsie.github.io/guizero**, including options for installing when you have no administration rights to your computer and downloadable installations for Windows.

Hello World

Now that you have guizero installed, let's check that it's working and write a small 'hello world' app which is traditional for programmers to write as their first program when using a new tool or language.

AIMS OF GUIZERO

- Able to be used without installation
- Remove unnecessary code new learners find difficult to understand
- Sensible widget names
- Accessible to young children, but able be used for advanced projects
- Good-quality documentation with examples
- Generate helpful error messages

Open up the editor where you will write your Python code. At the start of every guizero program, you will choose the widgets you need from the guizero library and import them. You only need to import each widget once, and then you can use it in your program as many times as you like.

At the top of the page, add this code to import the App widget:

```
from guizero import App
```

▲ **Figure 1** Your first guizero app

All guizero projects begin with a main window which is a container widget called an App. At the end of every guizero program, you must tell the program to display the app you have just created.

Add these two lines of code underneath the line where you imported the App widget:

```
app = App(title="Hello world")
app.display()
```

Now save and run your code. You should see a GUI window with the title 'Hello world' (**Figure 1**). Congratulations, you've just created your first guizero app!

Adding widgets

Widgets are the things which appear on the GUI, such as text boxes, buttons, sliders, and even plain old pieces of text.

All widgets go between the line of code to create the App and the `app.display()` line. Here is the app you just made, but in this example we have added a Text widget:

```
from guizero import App, Text
app = App(title="Hello world")
message = Text(app, text="Welcome to the app")
app.display()
```

Did you notice that there are two changes (**Figure 2**)? There is now an extra line of code to add the Text widget, and we have also added Text to the list of widgets to import on the very first line.

Let's look at the Text widget code in a bit more detail:

```
message = Text(app, text="Welcome to the app")
```

Just like any variable in Python, a widget needs a name. This one is called 'message'. Then we specify that we would like this to be a 'Text' widget. Inside the brackets are some parameters to tell the Text widget what it should look like. The first one, 'app', tells the Text where it will live. All widgets need to live inside a container widget. Most of the time your widgets will live directly inside an App, but you will discover later that there are also some other types of container widget you can put things in too. Finally, we tell the widget to contain the text "Welcome to the app".

🔺 **Figure 2** Add a text message

01-helloworld.py / Python 3

```
from guizero import App, Text
app = App(title="Hello world")
message = Text(app, text="Welcome to the app")
app.display()
```

magpi.cc/guizerocode

Chapter 2
Wanted Poster
Use styled text and an image to create a poster

Now that you can create a basic GUI, let's make it look a bit more exciting. You can add text in different fonts, sizes and colours, change the background colour, and add pictures too. To practise all of this, let's create a 'Wanted' poster.

First of all, you need to start off by creating an app. In your editor, add this code to create the most basic app window:

```python
from guizero import App

app = App("Wanted!")

app.display()
```

Save and run your code and you should see an app that looks like a plain grey square with the title 'Wanted!' at the top (**Figure 1**).

▲ **Figure 1** The basic app

CREATE GRAPHICAL USER INTERFACES WITH PYTHON

Background colours

Let's make the background of the app a bit different. Tra they are made of parchment, so let's add a pale yellow colour instead as the background.

Find the line of code where you create the app. Immediately after this line of code, add one more line of code to modify the bg property of the window. In this case, bg is short for 'background' and will let us change the colour of the background. Now your code should look like this:

```
from guizero import App

app = App("Wanted!")
app.bg = "yellow"

app.display()
```

▲ **Figure 2** Background colour

This is called editing a property. In the code, you need to specify the widget you are talking about (app), the property you want to change (bg) and the value you want to change it to.

You might think this colour (**Figure 2**) is a bit too yellow, so let's look up the hex code of a different yellow colour. There are lots of websites where you can search for colours, for example you could try **htmlcolorcodes.com** (**Figure 3**).

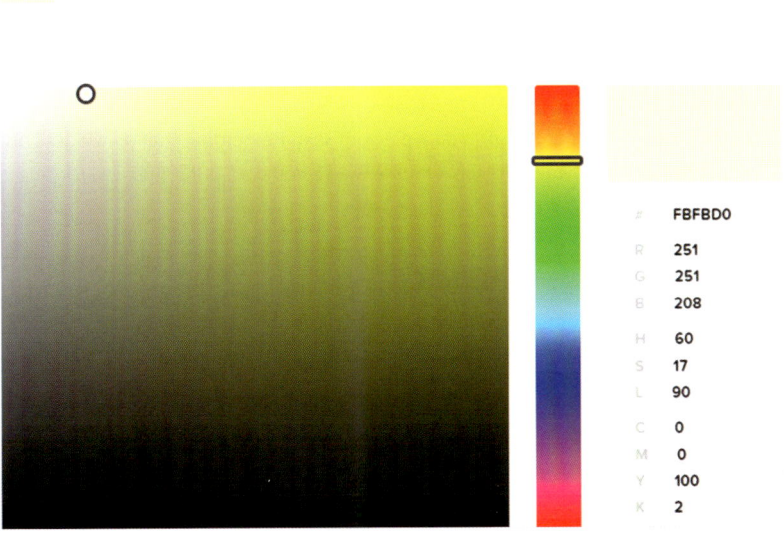

▲ **Figure 3** Selecting a shade on htmlcolorcodes.com

Chapter 2 Wanted Poster   13

When you have selected the colour you want, you will see its code displayed on the site either as hexadecimal (in this case #FBFBD0) or as RGB (251, 251, 208). You can use both of these formats for setting colours in guizero; for example, you could delete the code for making your background yellow and then try one of these options in your program:

```
app.bg = "#FBFBD0"
app.bg = (251, 251, 208)
```

▲ **Figure 4** Pale background

Add some text

Your app should look something like **Figure 4**. Now let's add some text to the GUI. We will begin by adding the text that all good wanted posters need – the word 'Wanted'!

First, look for the line of code you already have where you imported the App.

```
from guizero import App
```

You need to import Text to be able to create a piece of text, so add it to the end of the list. Now the line looks like this:

```
from guizero import App, Text
```

Every time you want to use a new type of widget, add its name to the end of the list. There is no need to keep adding whole new lines of code: just stick with one list so that your program doesn't get too confusing.

Now that you can use text, let's add a piece of text. Remember that all widgets on the GUI must be added between the line of code where you create the App and the line of code where you display it. Your code should now look like this:

```
from guizero import App, Text

app = App("Wanted!")
app.bg = "#FBFBD0"

wanted_text = Text(app, "WANTED")

app.display()
```

Let's take a closer look at that line of code you just added.

```
wanted_text = Text(app, "WANTED")
```

Here, `wanted_text` is the name of the piece of text. This is so that we can talk about it later on in the code – think of it like a person's name. (You could even call your piece of text Dave if you want – the computer won't care!)

Inside the brackets we have two things. The second one, `"WANTED"`, is straightforward as it is the text we would like to display on the screen. The first is the container which controls this piece of text, which is called its 'master'. In this case we are saying that this text should be controlled by the app. When you first start creating GUIs, most of your widgets will have the app as their master, but there are other containers that can store widgets that you will learn about later on.

Change text size and colour

Uh oh, this text is pretty small (**Figure 5**). Let's change the `text_size` property in exactly the same way as you did when we changed the background colour of the app. Remember that you needed to specify three things:

1. The name of the widget
2. Which property to change
3. The new value to change it to

So, in this case you are going to specify the widget (`wanted_text`), the property to change (`text_size`)

▲ **Figure 5** Text is too small

and the new value (`50`). Add one new line of code immediately under the line where you created the text, to change the property.

```
wanted_text = Text(app, "WANTED")
wanted_text.text_size = 50
```

You now have larger text on your poster (**Figure 6**). See if you can now change the font of this text to something different. Which fonts are available depends on which operating system you are using, so here are some suggestions:

- Times New Roman
- Verdana
- Courier
- Impact

▲ **Figure 6** Larger text

No 'wanted' poster would be complete without a picture, so let's add one. My poster is going to be for my cat, because she is always scratching things she shouldn't be.

Save a copy of the image you would like to use in the same folder as your GUI program. You can use images in other folders, but if you do you will have to provide the path to the image, so it's a lot easier to just store them in the same folder when you are starting out.

> **IMAGE MANIPULATION**
>
> Because guizero is a library for beginners and we wanted to make it as easy as possible to install, it does not come with the fancier image manipulation functions as these require an extra library called 'pillow'. You can always use non-animated GIF images on any platform, and PNG images on all platforms except Mac, so if you're not sure whether you have installed the extra image manipulation functions, stick to those image types.

Hopefully you're now getting used to adding widgets. Remember that they must always be imported at the top of the program, and then the widget created with a sensible name after the line of code where you create the App, but before the final `app.display()` line.

Add 'Picture' to the list of widgets to import at the start of the program.

```
from guizero import App, Text, Picture
```

Now create a Picture widget with two parameters: the app and the file name of the picture. This is the code we used because our picture was called **tabitha.png**.

```
cat = Picture(app, image="tabitha.png")
```

Run your code (which should look like **02-wanted.py**) again and you should see the picture displaying below your text (**Figure 7**).

Now it's up to you to use your new GUI customisation skills to style your poster however you would like.

▲ **Figure 7** The finished poster

READING THE DOCS

You might be wondering how to find out what properties a particular widget has that you can change. Even if you are a complete beginner programmer, it is worth learning how to read documentation because it will let you use the full power of guizero and any other libraries you come across.

The guizero documentation can be found at **lawsie.github.io/guizero**. Once you are there, click on the widget you would like to change, and scroll down until you reach the properties section. For example, if you select 'Text' under the heading of widgets, you will see all of the properties of a piece of Text that you can possibly change. Documentation also often contains helpful snippets of code which show you how to use a particular property or method, so don't be scared of having a look through – you never know what you might learn!

02-wanted.py / Python 3

DOWNLOAD
magpi.cc/guizerocode

```python
from guizero import App, Text, Picture

app = App("Wanted!")
app.bg = "#FBFBD0"

wanted_text = Text(app, "WANTED")
wanted_text.text_size = 50
wanted_text.font = "Times New Roman"

cat = Picture(app, image="tabitha.png")

app.display()
```

Chapter 3
Spy Name Chooser
Make an interactive GUI application

So far you've learnt how to customise your GUI with a variety of different options. It's now time to get into the really interactive part and make a GUI application that actually responds to input from the user. Who could resist pushing a big red button to generate a super secret spy name?

▲ **Figure 1** Displaying the text in a window

Since you already know how to create an app, why not go ahead and create a basic window and add some text if you like? Here is some code to get you started, and this code also includes some comments (the lines that start with a #) to help you structure your program:

```
# Imports --------------
from guizero import App, Text

# Functions ------------
```

```
# App ------------------
app = App("TOP SECRET")

# Widgets ---------------
title = Text(app, "Push the red button to find out your spy 
name")

# Display ---------------
app.display()
```

Run this code and you should see a window with the text (**Figure 1**).

Add a button

Let's go ahead and add a button to the GUI. Add PushButton to your list of imports so that you can use buttons. (Be careful to use a capital B!)

Underneath the Text widget, but before the app displays, add a line of code to create a button.

```
button = PushButton(app, choose_name, text="Tell me!")
```

Your code should now look like **spy1.py** (page 22). Run it and no button will appear, but you'll see an error in the shell window:

```
NameError: name 'choose_name' is not defined
```

This is because **choose_name** is the name of a command which runs when the button is pressed. Most GUI components can have a command attached to them. For a button, attaching a command means "when the button is pressed, run

⬛ **Figure 2** You now have a button

this command." A GUI program works differently to other Python programs you might have written because the order in which the commands are run in the program depends entirely on the order in which the user presses the buttons, moves the sliders, ticks the boxes or interacts with whichever other widgets you are using. The actual command is almost always the name of a function to run.

Chapter 3 Spy Name Chooser   19

Create a function

Let's write the function `choose_name` so your button has something it can do when it is pressed.

Look at your program and find the functions section. This is where you should write all of the functions which will

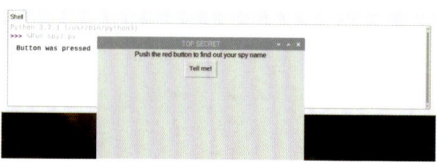

▲ **Figure 3** Text is output to the shell window

be attached to GUI widgets, to keep them separate from the code for displaying the widget. Add this code in the functions section:

```
def choose_name():
    print("Button was pressed")
```

Your code should now look like **spy2.py**. The button will now appear (**Figure 2**). If you press the button, it may appear that nothing has happened, but if you look in your shell or output window, you will see that some text has appeared there (**Figure 3**).

Instructing your function to first print out some dummy text is a useful way of confirming that the button is activating its command function correctly when it is pressed. You can then replace the `print` statement with the actual code for the task you would like your button to perform.

Inside your `choose_name` function, type a # symbol in front of the line of code that prints "Button was pressed". Programmers call this 'commenting out', and what you have done here is told the computer to treat this line of code as if it were a comment, or in other words you have instructed the computer to ignore it. The benefit of commenting a line of code out instead of just deleting it is so that if you ever want to use that code again, you can easily make it part of your program again by removing the # symbol.

BIG RED BUTTON

At the moment, your button is not big or red! You used properties in the previous chapter to change the appearance of your text on the 'Wanted' poster, so can you use the properties of the PushButton widget to change the background colour and the text size?

Note that it may not be possible to change the colour of a button on macOS, as some versions of the operating system will not allow you to do so, but you should still be able to alter the text size.

Add some names

On a new line, add a list of first names. You can choose the names in your list and there can be as many names as you like, but make sure that each name is between quotes, and the names are each separated by a comma. A collection of

▲ **Figure 4** Outputting a spy name

letters, numbers, and/or punctuation between quotation marks is called a *string*, so we say that each name must be a string.

```
first_names = ["Barbara", "Woody", "Tiberius", "Smokey",
"Jennifer", "Ruby"]
```

Now add a list of last names as well:

```
last_names = ["Spindleshanks", "Mysterioso", "Dungeon",
"Catseye", "Darkmeyer", "Flamingobreath"]
```

Now you will need to add a way of choosing a random name from each list to form your spy name. Your first job is to add a new import line in your imports section:

```
from random import choice
```

This tells the program that you would like to use a function called choice which chooses a random item from a list. Someone else has written the code which does this for you, and it is included with Python for you to use.

In your code for the `choose_name` function, just below your lists of names, add a line of code to choose your spy's first name, and then concatenate it together with the last name, with a space in between. Concatenate is a fancy word that means 'join two strings together' and the symbol in Python for concatenation is a plus (+).

```
spy_name = choice(first_names) + " " + choice(last_names)
print(spy_name)
```

Your code should now resemble **spy3.py**. Save and run it. When you press the button, you should see that a randomly generated spy name appears in your console or shell, in the same place where the original "Button was pressed" message showed up before (**Figure 4**).

Put the name in the GUI

That's good, but wouldn't it be nicer if the spy name appeared on the GUI? Let's make another Text widget and use it to display the spy name.

In the widgets section, add a new Text widget which will display the spy name:

⬛ **Figure 5** The finished spy name chooser

```
name = Text(app, text="")
```

When you create the widget, you don't want it to display any text at all as the person won't have pressed the button yet, so you can set the text to "", which is called an 'empty string' and displays nothing. Inside your `choose_name` function, comment out the line of code where you print out the spy name.

Now add a new line of code at the end of the function to set the value of the name Text widget to the `spy_name` you just created. This will cause the Text widget to update itself and display the name.

```
name.value = spy_name
```

Your final code should be as in **03-spy-name-chooser.py**. Run it and press the button to see your spy name displayed proudly on the GUI (**Figure 5**).

You can press the button again if you don't like the name you are given, and the program will randomly generate another name for you.

spy1.py / Python 3

⬇ **DOWNLOAD**

magpi.cc/guizerocode

```python
# Imports ---------------
from guizero import App, Text, PushButton

# Functions -------------

# App -------------------
app = App("TOP SECRET")

# Widgets ---------------
title = Text(app, "Push the red button to find out your spy name")
button = PushButton(app, choose_name, text="Tell me!")

# Display ---------------
app.display()
```

spy2.py / Python 3

```python
# Imports ---------------
from guizero import App, Text, PushButton

# Functions -------------
def choose_name():
    print("Button was pressed")

# App -------------------
app = App("TOP SECRET")

# Widgets ---------------
title = Text(app, "Push the red button to find out your spy name")
button = PushButton(app, choose_name, text="Tell me!")

# Display ---------------
app.display()
```

spy3.py / Python 3

```python
# Imports ---------------
from guizero import App, Text, PushButton
from random import choice

# Functions -------------
def choose_name():
    #print("Button was pressed")
    first_names = ["Barbara", "Woody", "Tiberius", "Smokey", "Jennifer", "Ruby"]
    last_names = ["Spindleshanks", "Mysterioso", "Dungeon", "Catseye", "Darkmeyer", "Flamingobreath"]
    spy_name = choice(first_names) + " " + choice(last_names)
    print(spy_name)

# App -------------------
app = App("TOP SECRET")

# Widgets ---------------
title = Text(app, "Push the red button to find out your spy name")
button = PushButton(app, choose_name, text="Tell me!")
button.bg = "red"
button.text_size = 30

# Display ---------------
app.display()
```

03-spy-name-chooser.py / Python 3

```python
# Imports ---------------

from guizero import App, Text, PushButton
from random import choice

# Functions -------------

def choose_name():
    #print("Button was pressed")
    first_names = ["Barbara", "Woody", "Tiberius", "Smokey", "Jennifer", "Ruby"]
    last_names = ["Spindleshanks", "Mysterioso", "Dungeon", "Catseye", "Darkmeyer", "Flamingobreath"]
    spy_name = choice(first_names) + " " + choice(last_names)
    #print(spy_name)
    name.value = spy_name

# App -------------------

app = App("TOP SECRET")

# Widgets ---------------

title = Text(app, "Push the red button to find out your spy name")
button = PushButton(app, choose_name, text="Tell me!")
button.bg = "red"
button.text_size = 30
name = Text(app, text="")

# Display ---------------

app.display()
```

Chapter 4
Meme Generator
Create a GUI application which draws memes

Let's take the lessons you learnt from the previous chapters to create a GUI which draws memes. You will input the text and image name and your GUI will combine them into your own meme using the Drawing widget.

Start by creating a simple GUI with two text boxes for the top and bottom text. This is where you will enter the text which will be inserted over your picture to create your meme. Add this line to import the widgets needed.

```
from guizero import App, TextBox, Drawing
```

Then add this code for the app:

```
app = App("meme")

top_text = TextBox(app, "top text")
bottom_text = TextBox(app, "bottom text")

app.display()
```

The meme will be created on a Drawing widget which will hold the image and text.

Create a meme

Add it to the GUI by inserting this code just before the `app.display()` line. The Drawing widget's height and width should be set to 'fill' the rest of the GUI.

```
meme = Drawing(app, width="fill", height="fill")
```

The meme will be created when the text in the top and bottom text boxes changes. To do that, we will need to create a function which draws the meme.

The function should clear the drawing, create an image (we're using a photo of a woodpecker, but you can use any you want) and insert the text at the top and bottom of the image.

Remember when you used `name.value` to set the value of the Text widget with the spy name in Chapter 3? You can also use the value property to *get* the value of a Text widget, so in this case `top_text.value` means 'please get the value that is typed in the top_text box'.

```
def draw_meme():
    meme.clear()
    meme.image(0, 0, "woodpecker.png")
    meme.text(20, 20, top_text.value)
    meme.text(20, 320, bottom_text.value)
```

The first two numbers in `meme.image(0, 0)` and `meme.text(20, 20)` are the x, y co-ordinates of where to draw the image and text. The image is drawn at position `0, 0`, which is the top-left corner, so the image covers the whole of the drawing.

Finally, call your `draw_meme` function just before you display the app. Insert this code just before the `app.display` line:

```
draw_meme()
```

Your code should now look like **meme1.py**.

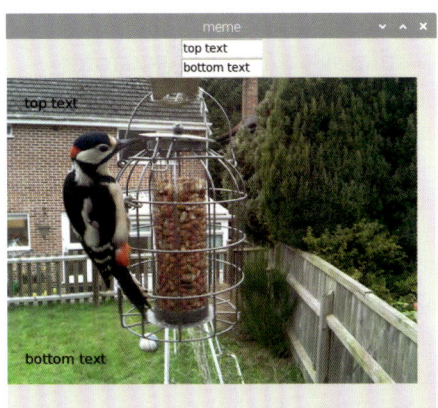

▲ **Figure 1** Meme with unstyled text

If you run your app (**Figure 1**) and try changing the top and bottom text, you will notice that it doesn't update in the meme. To get this working, you will have to change your program to call the `draw_meme` function when the text changes, by adding a command to the two TextBox widgets to the app.

```
top_text = TextBox(app, "top text", command=draw_meme)
bottom_text = TextBox(app, "bottom text", command=draw_meme)
```

Your code should now look like that in **meme2.py**. Run it and update your meme by changing the top and bottom text.

You can then look of your meme by changing the color, size, and font parameters of the text. For example:

```
meme.text(
    20, 20, top_text.value,
    color="orange",
    size=40,
    font="courier")
meme.text(
    20, 320, bottom_text.value,
    color="blue",
    size=28,
    font="times new roman",
    )
```

> **TIP**
>
> These lines of code were starting to get very long, so we have split them over a number of lines to make it easier to read. It doesn't affect what the program does, just how it looks.

Your code should now look like **meme3.py**. Try different styles until you find something you like (**Figure 2**).

Customise your meme generator

For a truly interactive meme generator, the user should be able to set the font, size, and colour themselves. You can provide additional widgets on the GUI to allow them to do this.

The number of options available for the colour and font are limited, so you could use a drop-down list, also known as a Combo, for this. The size could be set using a Slider widget.

▲ **Figure 2** Alter the fonts and colours

28 CREATE GRAPHICAL USER INTERFACES WITH PYTHON

First, modify your import statement to include the Combo and Slider widgets.

```
from guizero import App, TextBox, Drawing, Combo, Slider
```

After you have created your TextBox widgets for the top and bottom text, create a new Combo widget so the user can select a colour.

```
bottom_text = TextBox(app, "bottom text", command=draw_meme)
color = Combo(app,
    options=["black", "white", "red", "green", "blue", "orange"],
    command=draw_meme)
```

The **options** parameter sets what colours the user can select from the Combo. Each colour is an element in a list. You can add any other colours you want to the list.

The options are displayed in the order in which you put them in the list. The first option is the default, which is displayed first. If you want to have a different option as the default, you can do it using the **selected** parameter, e.g. **"blue"**.

```
color = Combo(app,
    options=["black", "white", "red", "green", "blue", "orange"],
    command=draw_meme,
    selected="blue")
```

Now your user can select a colour. Next, you need to change the **draw_meme** function to use Combo's value when creating the text in your the meme. For example:

```
meme.text(
    20, 20, top_text.value,
    color=color.value,
    size=40,
    font="courier")
```

Do the same for the bottom-text block of code. Your program should now resemble **meme4.py**.

Following the steps above, add a second Combo to your application so the user can select a font from this list of options: **["times new roman", "verdana", "courier", "impact"]**. Remember to change the **draw_meme** function to use the **font** value when adding the text.

Create a new Slider widget to set the size of the text your user wants.

```
size = Slider(app, start=20, end=40, command=draw_meme)
```

The range of the slider is set using the start and end parameters. So, in this example, the smallest text available will be 20 and the largest 40.

Modify the `draw_meme` function to use the value from your size slider when creating the meme's text.

```
meme.text(
    20, 20, top_text.value,
    color=color.value,
    size=size.value,
    font=font.value)
```

Your code should now resemble that in **04-meme-generator.py**. Try running it and you should see something like **Figure 3**.

Can you change the GUI so that the name of the image file can be entered into a TextBox or perhaps selected from a list in a Combo? This would make your application capable of generating memes with different images too.

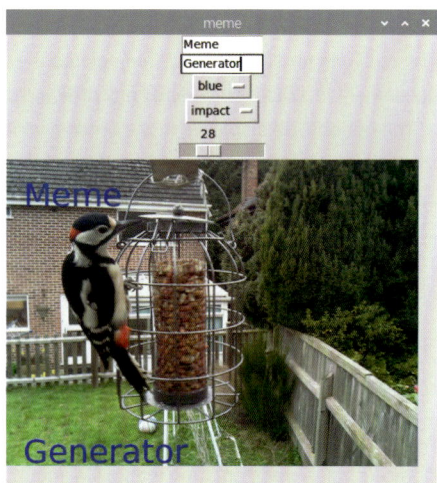

🔺 **Figure 3** The finished meme generator

DRAWING WIDGET

The Drawing widget is really versatile and can be used to display lots of different shapes, patterns, and images.

To find out more about the Drawing widget, see Appendix C, or take a look at the online documentation: **lawsie.github.io/guizero/drawing**.

CREATE GRAPHICAL USER INTERFACES WITH PYTHON

meme1.py / Python 3

⬇ DOWNLOAD
magpi.cc/guizerocode

```python
# Imports ---------------

from guizero import App, TextBox, Drawing


# Functions -------------

def draw_meme():
    meme.clear()
    meme.image(0, 0, "woodpecker.png")
    meme.text(20, 20, top_text.value)
    meme.text(20, 320, bottom_text.value)


# App -------------------

app = App("meme")

top_text = TextBox(app, "top text")
bottom_text = TextBox(app, "bottom text")

meme = Drawing(app, width="fill", height="fill")

draw_meme()

app.display()
```

meme2.py / Python 3

```python
# Imports ---------------

from guizero import App, TextBox, Drawing


# Functions -------------

def draw_meme():
    meme.clear()
    meme.image(0, 0, "woodpecker.png")
    meme.text(20, 20, top_text.value)
    meme.text(20, 320, bottom_text.value)
```

meme2.py (cont.) / Python 3

```python
# App ------------------

app = App("meme")

top_text = TextBox(app, "top text", command=draw_meme)
bottom_text = TextBox(app, "bottom text", command=draw_meme)

meme = Drawing(app, width="fill", height="fill")

draw_meme()

app.display()
```

meme3.py / Python 3

```python
# Imports ---------------

from guizero import App, TextBox, Drawing


# Functions -------------

def draw_meme():
    meme.clear()
    meme.image(0, 0, "woodpecker.png")
    meme.text(
        20, 20, top_text.value,
        color="orange",
        size=40,
        font="courier")
    meme.text(
        20, 320, bottom_text.value,
        color="blue",
        size=28,
        font="times new roman",
        )
```

meme3.py (cont.) / Python 3

```python
# App ------------------

app = App("meme")

top_text = TextBox(app, "top text", command=draw_meme)
bottom_text = TextBox(app, "bottom text", command=draw_meme)

meme = Drawing(app, width="fill", height="fill")

draw_meme()

app.display()
```

meme4.py / Python 3

```python
# Imports ---------------

from guizero import App, TextBox, Drawing, Combo, Slider


# Functions -------------

def draw_meme():
    meme.clear()
    meme.image(0, 0, "woodpecker.png")
    meme.text(
        20, 20, top_text.value,
        color=color.value,
        size=40,
        font="courier")
    meme.text(
        20, 320, bottom_text.value,
        color=color.value,
        size=28,
        font="times new roman",
        )


# App ------------------
```

meme4.py (cont.) / Python 3

```python
app = App("meme")

top_text = TextBox(app, "top text", command=draw_meme)
bottom_text = TextBox(app, "bottom text", command=draw_meme)

color = Combo(app,
              options=["black", "white", "red", "green", "blue", "orange"],
              command=draw_meme, selected="blue")

meme = Drawing(app, width="fill", height="fill")

draw_meme()

app.display()
```

04-meme-generator.py / Python 3

```python
# Imports ---------------

from guizero import App, TextBox, Drawing, Combo, Slider


# Functions -------------

def draw_meme():
    meme.clear()
    meme.image(0, 0, "woodpecker.png")
    meme.text(
        20, 20, top_text.value,
        color=color.value,
        size=size.value,
        font=font.value)
    meme.text(
        20, 320, bottom_text.value,
        color=color.value,
        size=size.value,
        font=font.value,
        )
```

04-meme-generator.py / Python 3

```python
# App -------------------

app = App("meme")

top_text = TextBox(app, "top text", command=draw_meme)
bottom_text = TextBox(app, "bottom text", command=draw_meme)

color = Combo(app,
              options=["black", "white", "red", "green", "blue", "orange"],
              command=draw_meme, selected="blue")

font = Combo(app,
             options=["times new roman", "verdana", "courier", "impact"],
             command=draw_meme)

size = Slider(app, start=20, end=50, command=draw_meme)

meme = Drawing(app, width="fill", height="fill")

draw_meme()

app.display()
```

Chapter 5
World's Worst GUI

Learn good GUI design by doing it all wrong first!

Its time to really go to town with your GUIs and experiment with different widgets, **colours, fonts, and features.** Like most experiments, it's likely that you won't get it right first time! In fact, you are going to explore the wrong way to approach creating your GUI.

It's hard to read

The right choice of GUI colour and font are important. It's important that the contrast between background and text colour ensure that your GUI is easily readable. What you shouldn't do it is use two very similar colours.

Import the widgets at the top of the code:

```
from guizero import App, Text
```

Create an app with a title:

```
app = App("it's all gone wrong")
title = Text(app, text="Some hard to read text")
```

```
app.display()
```

Experiment by changing the colours, font, and text size (see **worst1.py** listing, page 41). My choices are not the best!

```
app = App("it's all gone wrong", bg="dark green")
title = Text(app, text="Some hard-to-read text", size="14",
font="Comic Sans", color="green")
```

It's important that text on a GUI also stays around long enough to be read. It certainly shouldn't disappear or start flashing.

All widgets in guizero can be made invisible (or visible again) using the `hide()` and `show()` functions. Using the `repeat` function in guizero to run a function every second, you can make your text hide and show itself and appear to flash.

Create a function which will hide the text if it's visible and show it if it's not:

```
def flash_text():
    if title.visible:
        title.hide()
    else:
        title.show()
```

Before the app is displayed, use `repeat` to make the `flash_text` function run every 1000 milliseconds (1 second).

```
app.repeat(1000, flash_text)

app.display()
```

Your code should now look like **worst2.py**. Test your app: the title text should flash, appearing and disappearing once every second.

The wrong widget

Using an appropriate widget can be the difference between a great GUI and one which is completely unusable.

Which widget would you use to enter a date? A TextBox? Multiple Combos? A TextBox would be more flexible but would require validation and formatting. Multiple Combos for year, month, and day wouldn't require validating but would be slower to use.

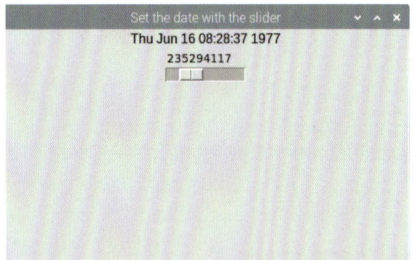

▲ **Figure 1** A slider to set date and time

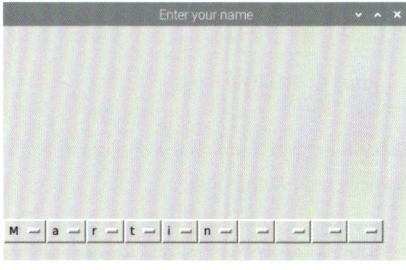

▲ **Figure 2** Combos to choose letters

Using a Slider to set a date and time (**Figure 1**), as in the **worst3.py** code example, is not a great idea, though.

The Slider widget returns a number between 0 and 999,999,999. This is the number of seconds since 1 January 1970. The function `ctime()` is used to turn this number into a date and time.

Getting text from your user is simple: a TextBox or a multi-line TextBox should fulfil all your needs. Is it too simple, though. Does this require too much typing?

What about the user who just wants to use a mouse? Perhaps a series of Combos each containing all the letters in the alphabet would be better (**Figure 2**)?

Start by importing the guizero widgets and `ascii_letters`.

```
from guizero import App, Combo
from string import ascii_letters
```

`ascii_letters` is a list containing all the 'printable' ASCII characters which you can use as the options for the Combo.

Create a single Combo which contains all the letters and displays the app.

```
a_letter = Combo(app, options=" " + ascii_letters, align="left")

app.display()
```

Your program should now resemble **worst4.py**. Running it, you will see a single Combo which contains all the letters plus a space and is aligned to the left of the window.

To get a line of letters together, you could continually add Combo widgets to your app, e.g.:

```
a_letter = Combo(app, options=" " + ascii_letters, align="left")
b_letter = Combo(app, options=" " + ascii_letters, align="left")
c_letter = Combo(app, options=" " + ascii_letters, align="left")
```

By aligning each Combo widget to the left, the widgets are displayed next to each other against the left edge.

Alternatively, you could use a **for** loop, create a list of letters, and append each letter to the list, as shown in **worst5.py**.

Try both these approaches and see which you prefer. The **for** loop is more flexible as it allows you to create as many letters as you like.

Pop-ups

No terrible GUI would be complete without a pop-up box. guizero contains a number of pop-up boxes, which can be used to let users know something important or gather useful information. They can also be used to irritate and annoy users!

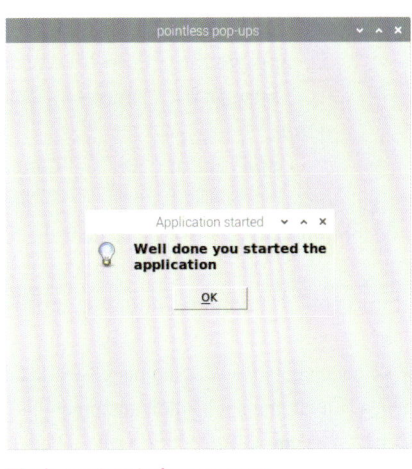

🔺 **Figure 3** Pointless pop-up

First, create an application which pops up a pointless box at the start to let you know the application has started.

```
from guizero import App

app = App(title="pointless pop-ups")

app.info("Application started", "Well done you started the application")

app.display()
```

Running your application, you will see that an 'info' box appears (**Figure 3**). The first parameter passed to info is the title of the window; the second parameter is the message.

You can change the style of this simple pop-up by using **warn** or **error** instead of **info**.

Pop-up boxes can also be used to get information from the user. The simplest is a **yesno** which will ask the user a question and get a True or False response. This is useful if you want a user to confirm before doing something, such as deleting a file. Perhaps not every time they press a button, though!

Import the PushButton widget into your application:

```
from guizero import App, PushButton
```

Create a function which uses the **yesno** pop-up to ask for confirmation.

```
def are_you_sure():
    if app.yesno("Confirmation", "Are you sure?"):
        app.info("Thanks", "Button pressed")
    else:
        app.error("Ok", "Cancelling")
```

Add the button to your GUI which calls the function when it is pressed.

```
button = PushButton(app, command=are_you_sure)
```

Your code should now resemble **05-worlds-worst-gui.py**. When you run the application and press the button, you will see a pop-up asking to you confirm with a Yes or No (**Figure 4**).

You can find out more about the pop-up boxes in guizero at **lawsie.github.io/guizero/alerts**.

How about combining all of these 'features' into one great GUI?

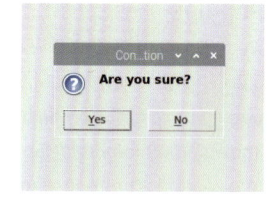

▲ **Figure 4** Yes, we're sure!

WINDOW WIDGET

Pop-up boxes can be used to ask users questions, but they are really simple.

If you want to do show additional information or ask for supplementary data, you could use the Window widget to create multiple windows.

Window is used in a similar way to App and has many of the same functions.

```
from guizero import App, Window

app = App("Main window")
window = Window(app, "2nd Window")

app.display()
```

You can control whether a Window is on screen using the `show()` and `hide()` methods.

```
window.show()
window.hide()
```

An app can be made to wait for a window to be closed after it has been shown, by passing True to the `wait` parameter of `show`. For example:

```
window.show(wait=True)
```

You can find out more about how to use multiple windows in the guizero documentation: **lawsie.github.io/guizero/multiple_windows**.

worst1.py / Python 3

⬇ **DOWNLOAD**

magpi.cc/guizerocode

```python
# Imports --------------

from guizero import App, Text


# App ------------------

app = App("its all gone wrong", bg="dark green")

title = Text(app, text="Hard to read", size="14", font="Comic Sans", color="green")

app.display()
```

worst2.py / Python 3

```python
# Imports --------------

from guizero import App, Text


# Functions -------------

def flash_text():
    if title.visible:
        title.hide()
    else:
        title.show()


# App ------------------

app = App("its all gone wrong", bg="dark green")

title = Text(app, text="Hard to read", size="14", font="Comic Sans", color="green")

app.repeat(1000, flash_text)

app.display()
```

worst3.py / Python 3

```python
# Imports ---------------

from guizero import App, Slider, Text
from time import ctime


# Functions -------------

def update_date():
    the_date.value = ctime(date_slider.value)


# App -------------------

app = App("Set the date with the slider")
the_date = Text(app)
date_slider = Slider(app, start=0, end=999999999, command=update_date)

app.display()
```

worst4.py / Python 3

```python
# Imports ---------------
from guizero import App, Combo
from string import ascii_letters


# App -------------------

app = App("Enter your name")

a_letter = Combo(app, options=" " + ascii_letters, align="left")

app.display()
```

worst5.py / Python 3

```python
# Imports ---------------

from guizero import App, Combo
from string import ascii_letters


# App ------------------

app = App("Enter your name")

name_letters = []
for count in range(10):
    a_letter = Combo(app, options=" " + ascii_letters, align="left")
    name_letters.append(a_letter)

app.display()
```

05-worlds-worst-gui.py / Python 3

```python
from guizero import App, PushButton

def are_you_sure():
    if app.yesno("Confirmation", "Are you sure?"):
        app.info("Thanks", "Button pressed")
    else:
        app.error("Ok", "Cancelling")

app = App(title="pointless pop-ups")

button = PushButton(app, command=are_you_sure)

app.info("Application started", "Well done you started the application")

app.display()
```

Chapter 6
Tic-tac-toe

Use your GUI to control a simple game

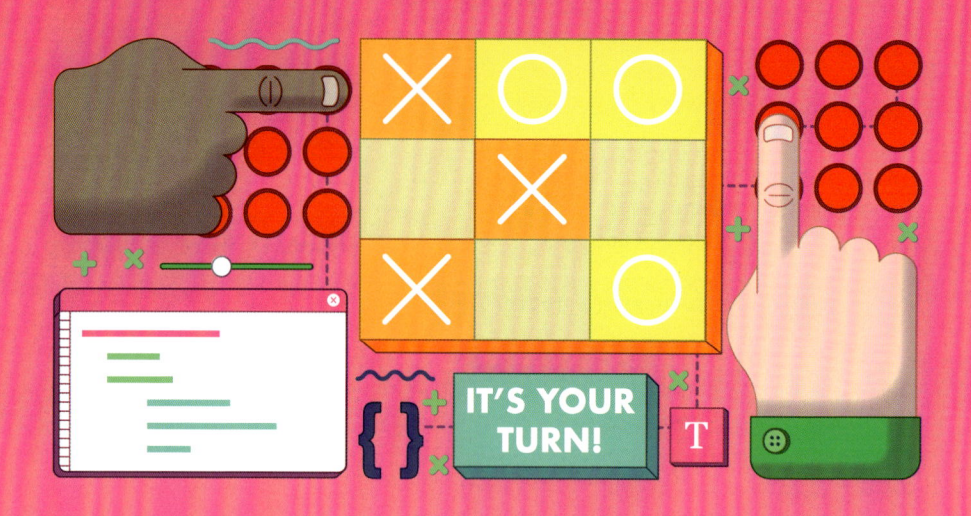

Now that you have learnt how to make a basic GUI, let's add some more programming logic behind the scenes to make your GUI work as the means of controlling a game of tic-tac-toe (also known as noughts and crosses).

Create a new file with the following code:

```
# Imports ---------------
from guizero import App

# Functions -------------

# Variables -------------

# App -------------------
app = App("Tic tac toe")

app.display()
```

CREATE GRAPHICAL USER INTERFACES WITH PYTHON

Create the board

Let's begin by creating the widgets which will make up the game board. A traditional tic-tac-toe board looks like the one shown in **Figure 1**.

You'll use buttons to represent each of the positions on the board, so that the player can click on one of the buttons indicating where they would like to move. To be able to lay out the buttons on a grid, let's create a new type of guizero widget called a Box.

A Box is a container widget. This means that it is used for containing other widgets and grouping them together. Add it to the imports at the top of your code:

▲ **Figure 1** A typical game of tic-tac-toe

```
from guizero import App, Box,
```

Set the Box to have a grid layout and add it to your app – before the `app.display()` line, as with all widgets.

```
board = Box(app, layout="grid")
```

If you run your program at this point, you won't see anything on the screen because the Box itself is invisible.

Now let's create the buttons to go inside it. You will need nine buttons in total, so instead of creating them individually, you can use a nested loop to generate them all automatically and give them co-ordinates. First, add PushButton to your list of widgets to import and then add this code immediately after the code for the board you just created.

```
for x in range(3):
    for y in range(3):
        button = PushButton(
            board, text="", grid=[x, y], width=3
        )
```

Chapter 6 Tic-tac-toe | 45

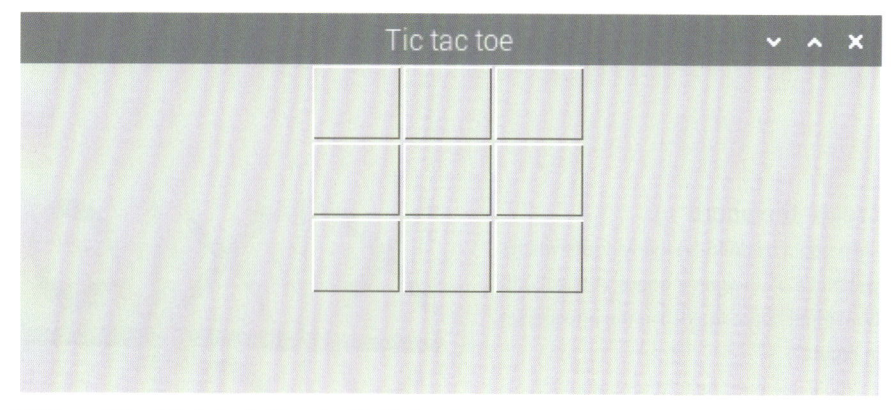

▲ **Figure 2** A grid of nine buttons to play tic-tac-toe

Notice that there are two loop variables: **x** from 0 to 2 and **y** from 0 to 2. As we iterate and generate buttons, each button will be added to the board, which is the Box container you created earlier. The button will be given the grid co-ordinates **x,y**, meaning that each button is neatly placed on a grid at a different position!

Your code should now look like **tictactoe1.py**. The result of running it is shown in **Figure 2**.

Underlying data structure

You might notice that when you create the buttons using a loop, you are creating nine buttons automatically and every single one is called `button`. How will you be able to refer to each of these buttons in the program?

The answer is that you need an underlying data structure to hold a reference to each button, and for this you will use a two-dimensional list.

Let's create a function which we can call to clear the board. It is a good idea to do this in a function so that you can reuse the code once the game has been played to reset the board and allow the player to begin a fresh game.

In the functions section, add a new function called `clear_board`.

```
def clear_board():
```

Your first job inside this function is to initialise the data structure for the board. Let's assume at this point you have not created any buttons, so you can initialise each position on the board as **None** – the element in the list now exists but does not yet have a value. Add the following line, indented, to your function.

```
new_board = [[None, None, None], [None, None, None], [None, None, None]]
```

Next, move the nested loop code from your app section into the **clear_board** function. Make sure the indentation is correct.

Inside the inner (y) loop, add a line of code to store a reference to each button at its x,y co-ordinate position within the two-dimensional list so that you can refer to it later.

```
new_board[x][y] = button
```

Finally, after the loops end, return the **new_board** you have just created. Your function should look like this:

```
def clear_board():
    new_board = [[None, None, None],
                 [None, None, None],
                 [None, None, None]]
    for x in range(3):
        for y in range(3):
            button = PushButton(
                board, text="", grid=[x, y], width=3
            )
            new_board[x][y] = button
    return new_board
```

In the app section, initialise a list called **board_squares** and set it to call the new function you just created.

```
board_squares = clear_board()
```

This variable will be assigned the value of the **new_board** you created within the function, which should be a blank board with nine buttons. Make sure that you create this variable after the code for creating the Box, otherwise you will be trying to add buttons to a container that does not yet exist.

Your code will now resemble **tictactoe2.py**. Save and run the program and you should see an identical result to the one you had at the end of the last step, but now you have a hidden two-dimensional list data structure to let you reference and manipulate the buttons.

If you want to see what your 2D list looks like, you could add a **print** command to print the **board_squares** list: **print(board_squares)**. You should then see nine lots of **[PushButton] object with text ""** appear in the shell.

Make the buttons work

At the moment, your buttons don't do anything when you press them. Let's make a function to attach to the button, so that when it is pressed, the button displays either X or O depending on which player chose it.

First, create a variable in the variables section to record whose turn it is. You can choose to start with either player, but we will choose to start with X.

```
turn = "X"
```

This now means that you need to display on the GUI whose turn it is (**Figure 3**) so the players don't get confused. Add Text to your list of widgets to import:

```
from guizero import App, Box, PushButton, Text
```

Then add a new Text widget in the app section to display the turn.

```
message = Text(app, text="It is your turn, " + turn)
```

Move to the functions section and create a new function called `choose_square`.

```
def choose_square(x, y):
```

You will notice that this function takes two arguments – **x** and **y**. This is so that you know which square on the board has been clicked.

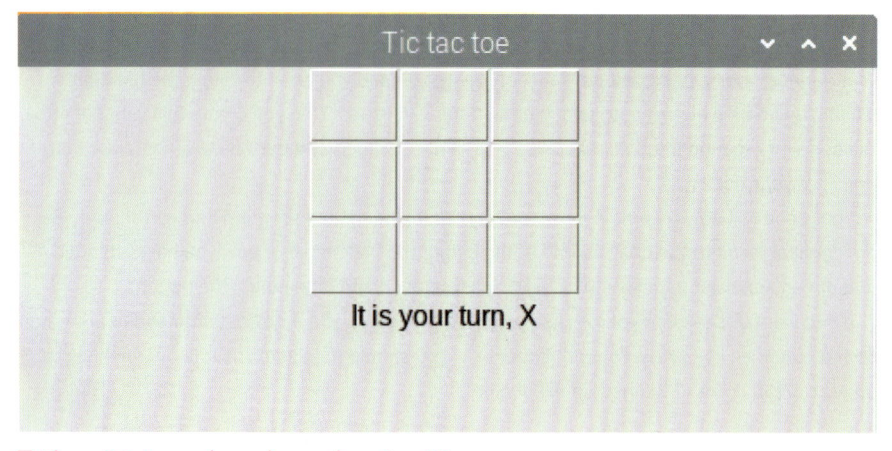

⬛ **Figure 3** Let your players know whose turn it is

Add the following code (indented) inside the function to set the text inside the button that was clicked to the symbol of the current player, and then disable the button so it cannot be clicked on again.

```
board_squares[x][y].text = turn
board_squares[x][y].disable()
```

Finally, connect this function to the button. Find this line of code inside your `clear_board` function:

```
button = PushButton(board, text="", grid=[x, y], width=3)
```

Modify it so that it looks like the line below:

```
button = PushButton(board, text="", grid=[x, y], width=3,
 command=choose_square, args=[x,y])
```

You have added two things here. Firstly, you are attaching a command, just as before. When the button is pressed, the function with this name will be called. Secondly, you are also providing arguments to this function, which are the co-ordinates x and y of the button which was pressed, so that you can find that button again in the list.

Your program should now look like **tictactoe3.py**. Save and run it. You will now be able to click on a button and it will change to an X. Unfortunately, in this version of the game it is permanently X's turn!

Alternating between players

Once one player has taken their turn, the turn variable should toggle to be the other player. Here is a function which will toggle from X to O and vice versa.

```
def toggle_player():
    global turn
    if turn == "X":
        turn = "O"
    else:
        turn = "X"
```

Add the code in your functions section. Notice the first line in the function: `global turn`. You need to specify this so that you are allowed to modify the *global* version of the `turn` variable, i.e. the one you already created. If you don't specify this, Python will create a local variable called `turn` and modify that instead, but that change won't be saved once the function exits.

You also need to make sure that the Text widget accurately reports the current player's turn. After the if/else statement in the **toggle_player** function, update the message like this:

```
message.value = "It is your turn, " + turn
```

Go back to your **choose_square** function and call the **toggle_player** function – with **toggle_player()** – once you have set the text and disabled the button. Your code should now resemble **tictactoe4.py**. Save and test the program again and you should find that you can click squares and they will alternately be designated either X or O.

Do we have a winner?

Finally, you need to write a function which will check whether there is a row, column, or diagonal of three Xs or Os, and if so will report the winner of the game.

Although it seems very inelegant, by far the easiest way to check if someone has won is to hard-code the checks for each vertical, horizontal, and diagonal line individually.

The following code is for one vertical line, one horizontal line, and one diagonal – can you add the rest?

```
def check_win():
    winner = None

    # Vertical lines
    if (
        board_squares[0][0].text == board_squares[0][1].text ==
board_squares[0][2].text
    ) and board_squares[0][2].text in ["X", "O"]:
        winner = board_squares[0][0]

    # Horizontal lines
    elif (
        board_squares[0][0].text == board_squares[1][0].text ==
board_squares[2][0].text
    ) and board_squares[2][0].text in ["X", "O"]:
        winner = board_squares[0][0]

    # Diagonals
    elif (
        board_squares[0][0].text == board_squares[1][1].text ==
board_squares[2][2].text
```

```
        ) and board_squares[2][2].text in ["X", "O"]:
            winner = board_squares[0][0]
```

Notice that the function begins by creating a Boolean variable called **winner**. If by the time the long if/elif statement has been executed, the value of this variable is True, you know that someone has won the game.

After adding the remaining winning line checks, add some code at the end of the function to change the display message if there has been a winner:

```
if winner is not None:
    message.value = winner.text + " wins!"
```

You now need to make sure that this function is called each time an X or O is placed, which corresponds to any time a button is pressed. Add a call to **check_win** at the end of the **choose_square** function, just in case the square that was chosen was the winning square.

Your program should now look like **tictactoe5.py**. Run it and test the game. If you wrote the tests in the **check_win** function correctly, you should find that the game detects correctly when a player has won.

RESET THE GAME

At the start, you wrote a function called **clear_board**. This may have seemed unnecessary at the time, but in actual fact it was thinking ahead to when the game has ended. Since tic-tac-toe is quite a short game, it is likely that someone might want to play more than one game in a row.

Can you add a reset button to your game, which only appears once either someone has won the game, or the game was a draw? The button should call the **clear_board** function and reset the **turn** variable as well as the message reporting whose turn it is.

Hint: You will need to check the guizero documentation to find out how to hide and show widgets, so that your button is not visible all of the time during the game.

Hint: Create a new function which takes care of everything you need to do to reset the game, and call that function when the reset button is pressed. Don't forget that in your function you'll need to specify some variables as global.

Draw game

At the moment, the game will allow you to continue playing even after it has been won, until all of the squares are selected. It will also not tell you if the game was a draw. You could stop at this point, but if you really want to put the icing on the cake, adding a few more little touches could make your game more polished.

First, let's add some code to detect whether the game is a draw. The game is a draw if all of the squares contain either an X or an O, and no one has won. In the functions section, create a new function called moves_taken:

```
def moves_taken():
```

You're going to use this function to count the number of moves which have been made, so let's start a variable to keep count, initially beginning at 0.

```
def moves_taken():
    moves = 0
```

Now, remember when we created the board_squares, we used a nested loop to create all of the squares on the grid? We're going to need another nested loop here to check each and every square and determine whether it has been filled in with an X or O, or whether it is blank.

> ### GLOBAL VARIABLES
>
> It is arguably a bad idea to use global variables because if you have many functions in a large program, it can become extremely confusing as to which code modifies the value of a variable and when. In a small program like this, it is not too difficult to keep track.
>
> Remember that it is possible to read and use the value of a global variable from inside a function without declaring it global, but in order to modify its value you will need to explicitly declare this. The functions in this program (and most GUI programs in this book) are actually modifying the values of your widgets as global variables. For example, when someone wins the game, you set the value of the message to display who won:
>
> `message.value = winner.text + " wins!"`
>
> In this example, message is a global variable. So how can we modify its value without declaring it as global? The answer is because we are using a *property* of the `message` widget, the property called value. Essentially what this code is saying is "Hey Python, you know that widget over there called message? Well, could you modify its value property please?" Python will allow modification through object properties in the global scope, but it won't allow you to directly modify the value of a variable without declaring it global.

Add this code for a nested loop to the **moves_taken** function:

```
for row in board_squares:
    for col in row:
```

Inside the loop, we need to check whether that particular square is filled in with an X or an O. If it is, add 1 to the **moves** variable to record that square has been counted.

```
if col.text == "X" or col.text == "O":
    moves = moves + 1
```

Finally, once the loops have finished, add a **return** statement to return the number of moves taken.

```
return moves
```

Now, call this function inside the **check_win** function, to check for a draw. Add this code after the code that checks for a winner:

```
if winner is not None:
    message.value = winner.text + " wins!"

# Add this code
elif moves_taken() == 9:
    message.value = "It's a draw"
```

Your code should resemble **06-tictactoe.py**. When run, the game will now check whether nine moves have been taken; if they have, it will change the message to report that the game was a draw.

tictactoe1.py / Python 3

DOWNLOAD
magpi.cc/guizerocode

```python
# Imports ---------------
from guizero import App, Box, PushButton

# Functions -------------

# Variables -------------

# App -------------------
app = App("Tic tac toe")

board = Box(app, layout="grid")
for x in range(3):
    for y in range(3):
        button = PushButton(board, text="", grid=[x, y], width=3)

app.display()
```

tictactoe2.py / Python 3

```python
# Imports ---------------
from guizero import App, Box, PushButton

# Functions -------------
def clear_board():
    new_board = [[None, None, None], [None, None, None], [None, None, None]]
    for x in range(3):
        for y in range(3):
            button = PushButton(
                board, text="", grid=[x, y], width=3)
            new_board[x][y] = button
    return new_board

# Variables -------------

# App -------------------
app = App("Tic tac toe")

board = Box(app, layout="grid")
board_squares = clear_board()

app.display()
```

tictactoe3.py / Python 3

```python
# Imports ---------------
from guizero import App, Box, PushButton, Text

# Functions -------------
def clear_board():
    new_board = [[None, None, None], [None, None, None], [None, None, None]]
    for x in range(3):
        for y in range(3):
            button = PushButton(board, text="", grid=[x, y], width=3, command=choose_square, args=[x,y])
            new_board[x][y] = button
    return new_board

def choose_square(x, y):
    board_squares[x][y].text = turn
    board_squares[x][y].disable()

# Variables -------------
turn = "X"

# App -------------------
app = App("Tic tac toe")

board = Box(app, layout="grid")
board_squares = clear_board()
message = Text(app, text="It is your turn, " + turn)

app.display()
```

tictactoe4.py / Python 3

```python
# Imports ---------------
from guizero import App, Box, PushButton, Text

# Functions -------------
def clear_board():
    new_board = [[None, None, None], [None, None, None], [None, None, None]]
    for x in range(3):
        for y in range(3):
            button = PushButton(board, text="", grid=[x, y], width=3, command=choose_square, args=[x,y])
            new_board[x][y] = button
    return new_board

def choose_square(x, y):
    board_squares[x][y].text = turn
    board_squares[x][y].disable()
    toggle_player()

def toggle_player():
    global turn
    if turn == "X":
        turn = "O"
    else:
        turn = "X"
    message.value = "It is your turn, " + turn

# Variables -------------
turn = "X"

# App -------------------
app = App("Tic tac toe")

board = Box(app, layout="grid")
board_squares = clear_board()
message = Text(app, text="It is your turn, " + turn)

app.display()
```

tictactoe5.py / Python 3

```python
# Imports ---------------
from guizero import App, Box, PushButton, Text

# Functions ------------
def clear_board():
    new_board = [[None, None, None], [None, None, None], [None, None, None]]
    for x in range(3):
        for y in range(3):
            button = PushButton(board, text="", grid=[x, y], width=3, command=choose_square, args=[x,y])
            new_board[x][y] = button
    return new_board

def choose_square(x, y):
    board_squares[x][y].text = turn
    board_squares[x][y].disable()
    toggle_player()
    check_win()

def toggle_player():
    global turn
    if turn == "X":
        turn = "O"
    else:
        turn = "X"
    message.value = "It is your turn, " + turn

def check_win():
    winner = None

    # Vertical lines
    if (
        board_squares[0][0].text == board_squares[0][1].text == board_squares[0][2].text
        ) and board_squares[0][2].text in ["X", "O"]:
        winner = board_squares[0][0]
    elif (
        board_squares[1][0].text == board_squares[1][1].text == board_squares[1][2].text
        ) and board_squares[1][2].text in ["X", "O"]:
        winner = board_squares[1][0]
    elif (
        board_squares[2][0].text == board_squares[2][1].text == board_squares[2][2].text
        ) and board_squares[2][2].text in ["X", "O"]:
```

tictactoe5.py (cont.) / Python 3

```python
            winner = board_squares[2][0]

    # Horizontal lines
    elif (
        board_squares[0][0].text == board_squares[1][0].text == board_squares[2][0].text
    ) and board_squares[2][0].text in ["X", "O"]:
        winner = board_squares[0][0]
    elif (
        board_squares[0][1].text == board_squares[1][1].text == board_squares[2][1].text
    ) and board_squares[2][1].text in ["X", "O"]:
        winner = board_squares[0][1]
    elif (
        board_squares[0][2].text == board_squares[1][2].text == board_squares[2][2].text
    ) and board_squares[2][2].text in ["X", "O"]:
        winner = board_squares[0][2]

    # Diagonals
    elif (
        board_squares[0][0].text == board_squares[1][1].text == board_squares[2][2].text
    ) and board_squares[2][2].text in ["X", "O"]:
        winner = board_squares[0][0]
    elif (
        board_squares[2][0].text == board_squares[1][1].text == board_squares[0][2].text
    ) and board_squares[0][2].text in ["X", "O"]:
        winner = board_squares[0][2]

    if winner is not None:
        message.value = winner.text + " wins!"

# Variables -------------
turn = "X"

# App -------------------
app = App("Tic tac toe")

board = Box(app, layout="grid")
board_squares = clear_board()
message = Text(app, text="It is your turn, " + turn)

app.display()
```

06-tictactoe.py / Python 3

```python
# Imports ---------------
from guizero import App, Box, PushButton, Text

# Functions -------------
def clear_board():
    new_board = [[None, None, None], [None, None, None], [None, None, None]]
    for x in range(3):
        for y in range(3):
            button = PushButton(board, text="", grid=[x, y], width=3, command=choose_square, args=[x,y])
            new_board[x][y] = button
    return new_board

def choose_square(x, y):
    board_squares[x][y].text = turn
    board_squares[x][y].disable()
    toggle_player()
    check_win()

def toggle_player():
    global turn
    if turn == "X":
        turn = "O"
    else:
        turn = "X"
    message.value = "It is your turn, " + turn

def check_win():
    winner = None

    # Vertical lines
    if (
        board_squares[0][0].text == board_squares[0][1].text == board_squares[0][2].text
    ) and board_squares[0][2].text in ["X", "O"]:
        winner = board_squares[0][0]
    elif (
        board_squares[1][0].text == board_squares[1][1].text == board_squares[1][2].text
    ) and board_squares[1][2].text in ["X", "O"]:
        winner = board_squares[1][0]
    elif (
        board_squares[2][0].text == board_squares[2][1].text == board_squares[2][2].text
```

Chapter 6 Tic-tac-toe

06-tictactoe.py (cont.) / Python 3

```python
        ) and board_squares[2][2].text in ["X", "O"]:
            winner = board_squares[2][0]

        # Horizontal lines
        elif (
            board_squares[0][0].text == board_squares[1][0].text ==
board_squares[2][0].text
        ) and board_squares[2][0].text in ["X", "O"]:
            winner = board_squares[0][0]
        elif (
            board_squares[0][1].text == board_squares[1][1].text ==
board_squares[2][1].text
        ) and board_squares[2][1].text in ["X", "O"]:
            winner = board_squares[0][1]
        elif (
            board_squares[0][2].text == board_squares[1][2].text ==
board_squares[2][2].text
        ) and board_squares[2][2].text in ["X", "O"]:
            winner = board_squares[0][2]

        # Diagonals
        elif (
            board_squares[0][0].text == board_squares[1][1].text ==
board_squares[2][2].text
        ) and board_squares[2][2].text in ["X", "O"]:
            winner = board_squares[0][0]
        elif (
            board_squares[2][0].text == board_squares[1][1].text ==
board_squares[0][2].text
        ) and board_squares[0][2].text in ["X", "O"]:
            winner = board_squares[0][2]

        if winner is not None:
            message.value = winner.text + " wins!"
        elif moves_taken() == 9:
            message.value = "It's a draw"

def moves_taken():
    moves = 0
    for row in board_squares:
        for col in row:
            if col.text == "X" or col.text == "O":
                moves = moves + 1
    return moves
```

06-tictactoe.py (cont.) / Python 3

```python
# Variables -------------
turn = "X"

# App ------------------
app = App("Tic tac toe")

board = Box(app, layout="grid")
board_squares = clear_board()
message = Text(app, text="It is your turn, " + turn)

app.display()
```

Chapter 7

Destroy the Dots

Learn how to use a Waffle to create a tasty game

You saw in the Tic-tac-toe game how to create a GUI on a grid layout in order to present the player with a grid-like board. If you are making a game involving a larger grid, there is a type of guizero widget called a Waffle which can instantly create a grid for you, and is really useful for creating all kinds of fun games.

A Waffle was originally a grid of squares in early versions of guizero. This game is called 'Destroy the dots' and it came about because Martin thought it was a good idea to allow a Waffle widget to contain a mixture of squares and dots.

Aim of the game

In this game, you need to destroy the dots before they destroy you! The board consists of a grid of squares. The squares will gradually turn into dots. To destroy a dot, click on the dot and it will turn back into a square. The aim of the game is to last as long as possible before being overrun by dots (**Figure 1**).

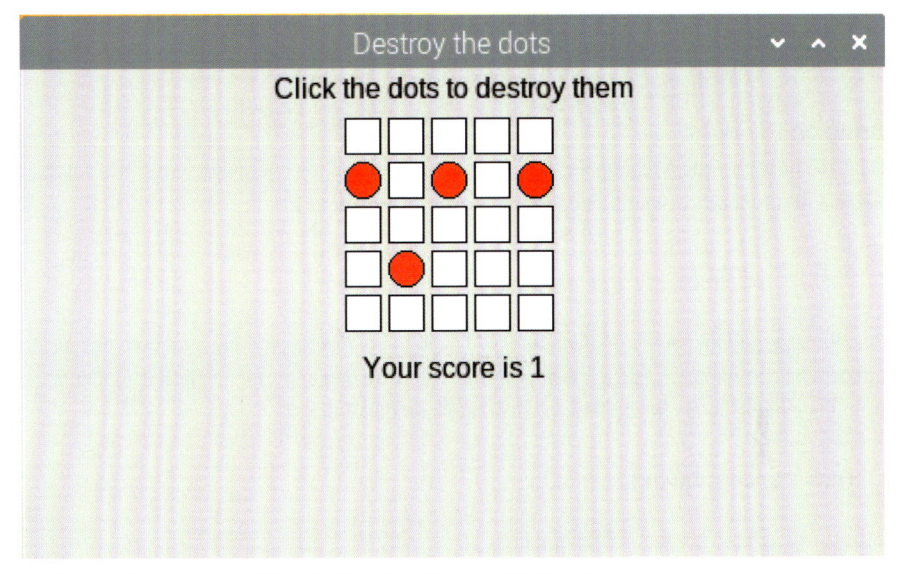

▲ Figure 1 Destroy the red dots before they take over the board

Set up the game

Let's start by making a guizero program which contains the instructions for the game and a Waffle. By now you should be familiar with the layout of a standard guizero program with sections for imports, functions, variables, and the app itself.

First, create an App and inside it add a Text widget for the instructions and a Waffle widget for the board:

```
# Imports ---------------
from guizero import App, Text, Waffle

# App -------------------
app = App("Destroy the dots")

instructions = Text(app, text="Click the dots to destroy them")
board = Waffle(app)

app.display()
```

If you run your program, you will see a small 3×3 grid of white squares. If you want to make your grid bigger than this, you can add width and height properties to your Waffle:

```
board = Waffle(app, width=5, height=5)
```

Your code should now resemble **destroy1.py** (page 71).

Bring on the dots

Next you need to write a function to find a random square on the board and turn it into a dot. Begin a new function in your functions section called **add_dot()**:

```
def add_dot():
```

To choose a random square on the board, you need to be able to generate a random pair of integers as co-ordinates. Add a line in your imports section to import the **randint** function from the **random** library, which lets you generate a random integer.

```
from random import randint
```

Let's generate two variables, **x** and **y**, which you can use to reference a co-ordinate on the grid. Inside your **add_dot()** function, begin your code like this:

```
x, y = randint(0,4), randint(0,4)
```

Notice that you have generated two random integers between 0 and 4, because earlier on you set the width and height of the grid to be 5 – the rows and columns will be numbered from 0. If you chose different values earlier on, you will need to adjust the values here to fit the size of your grid. However, there is a better way to manage aspects like this (see 'Using constants' box on page 70).

Dot or not?

Now that you know about constants, you can use the following function to generate a random co-ordinate on the grid:

```
def add_dot():
    x, y = randint(0,GRID_SIZE-1), randint(0,GRID_SIZE-1)
```

At this point, you don't know whether the randomly chosen co-ordinate is already a dot or not. This might not seem to make any difference at the start of a game when the board is mostly squares, but as the board gets filled up with dots, you need to make sure that the space is actually a square, otherwise the game will be too easy. One way to achieve this is to run a loop which checks whether the chosen square is already a dot, and if it is, chooses another random square:

CREATE GRAPHICAL USER INTERFACES WITH PYTHON

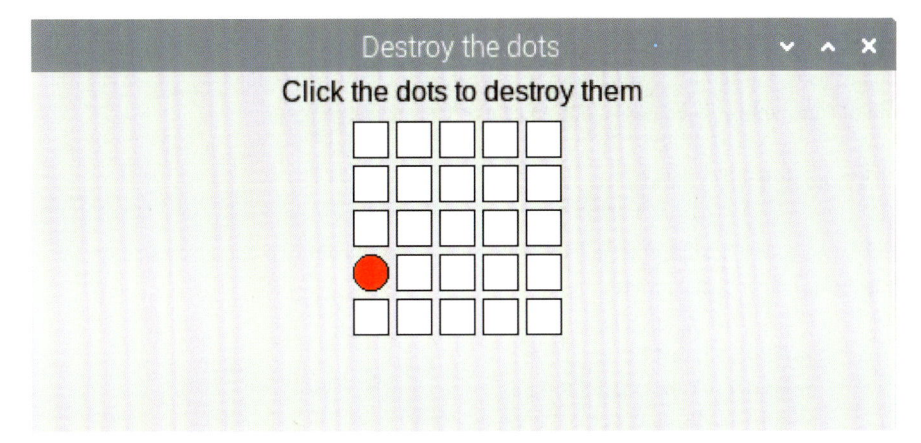

▲ **Figure 2** Generating a random red dot

```
x, y = randint(0,GRID_SIZE-1), randint(0,GRID_SIZE-1)
while board[x, y].dotty == True:
    x, y = randint(0,GRID_SIZE-1), randint(0,GRID_SIZE-1)
```

You might realise that this isn't a particularly efficient method of choosing a random square that is not a dot, but it will do for what we need in this game.

As soon as this loop finishes, you can be sure that the randomly chosen x, y co-ordinate is definitely a square. Let's convert it to a red dot – following (not inside) your **while** loop, add the following lines:

```
board[x, y].dotty = True
board.set_pixel(x, y, "red")
```

Add a call to your new **add_dot()** function in the app section after you've created the board. Your program should now resemble **destroy2.py**. When you run it, you should see a single random red dot in the grid. If you run the program again, the dot will probably be in a different random place (**Figure 2**).

Destroy the dot

So far there is only one dot – let's destroy it! Don't worry: you'll add more dots to destroy later on, but once you can destroy one, you can destroy them all!

Make a new function in your functions section with a really satisfying name – **destroy_dot** – and give it two parameters, **x** and **y**.

```
def destroy_dot(x, y):
```

This function will check whether the co-ordinate x,y is a dot (rather than a square). You can do this using the same code as the code to create a dot – the code `board[x, y].dotty` will return True if that coordinate is a dot, and False if it is a square.

```
if board[x,y].dotty == True:
```

If the co-ordinate is a dot, change it to a square by setting its `dotty` property to False, and also change its colour back to white:

```
if board[x,y].dotty == True:
    board[x,y].dotty = False
    board.set_pixel(x, y, "white")
```

This function needs to be triggered whenever the board is clicked. Find the line of code you already have which creates the board, and add a command like this:

```
board = Waffle(app, width=GRID_SIZE, height=GRID_SIZE, command=destroy_dot)
```

This will call the `destroy_dot` function whenever a space on the board is clicked.
   Note that a Waffle widget will automatically pass two parameters to any command function; these will always be the x and y co-ordinates of the pixel that was clicked on to trigger the command.
   Your code should now look like **destroy3.py**. Test your program by running it and clicking on the dot. You should see the dot turn back into a white square. If you click on a square that is not a dot, nothing should happen.

More dots!

Now it's time to actually make the game a challenge, by adding continually spawning dots. Let's start off by adding a new random dot every second. To do this, you need to schedule a call to the `add_dot` function every second using a built-in feature of guizero called `after`.
   In your app section, remove the call to `add_dot()` and replace it with a new line of code:

```
board.after(1000, add_dot)
```

This line of code means 'after 1000 milliseconds (1 second), call the function `add_dot`'.
   If you run the program now, you'll still get a single dot, but it will appear on the grid after a delay of 1 second.
   Here's the clever bit. Find your `add_dot` function and add the same line of code to it, at the end of the function.

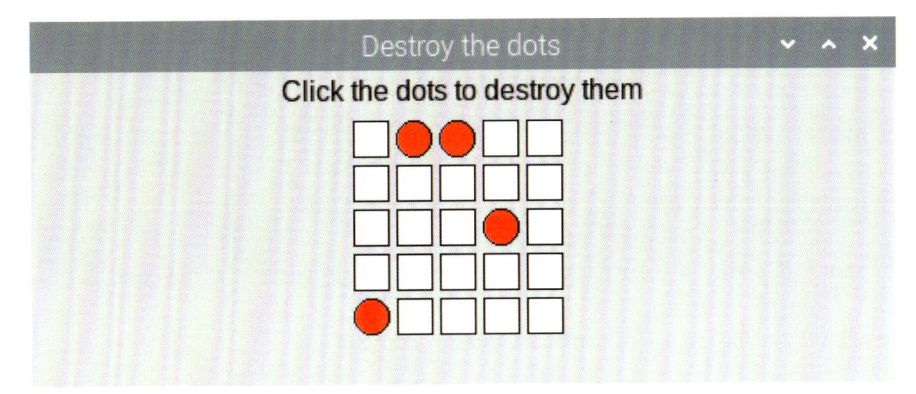

▲ Figure 3 Every second, a new dot will appear

This will schedule a new call to **add_dot** every time a new dot finishes being added. The next dot is scheduled to appear in 1 second as well, so if you run the program you should see a new dot appearing on the grid every second (**Figure 3**).

Try running your program, which should now look like **destroy4.py**. Since you already wrote the method to destroy a dot, clicking on any dot should remove it. However, if you play the game for a while you will notice it is pretty easy to keep up with the pace of one dot every second and it is almost impossible to lose the game.

You still need to add two things – a score to keep track of how many dots you have destroyed, and a way of making the game get more difficult so that it becomes a challenge.

Add a score

Adding a score is pretty straightforward and takes three steps:

- Add a variable to keep track of the score; the variable should start at 0.
- Display a message on the GUI with the current score.
- Any time the `destroy_dot` function is called and a dot is destroyed, add 1 to score and update the message display.

Try to add the code yourself using what you have already learnt.

Hint: To update the score variable from the `destroy_dot` function, you will need to declare it a global.

Hint: If you get an error saying that the variable score is referenced before assignment, make sure your variables section comes before your functions section in your program.

The solution is shown overleaf if you are stuck...

Solution: add a score

First, add a variable in your variables section

```
score = 0
```

Next, add a new Text widget in the app section to display the score:

```
score_display = Text(app, text="Your score is " + str(score))
```

Finally, add 1 to the score every time a dot is destroyed:

```
def destroy_dot(x,y):

    # Declare score global
    global score

    # This code already exists
    if board[x,y].dotty == True:
        board[x,y].dotty = False
        board.set_pixel(x, y, "white")

        # Add 1 to score and display it on the GUI
        score += 1
        score_display.value = "Your score is " + str(score)
```

Your code (without the optional comments) should now resemble **destroy5.py**. Test your game and you should see your score go up by 1 every time you click on a dot.

Put the player under pressure

Now that you can track the player's score, you can use it to put the player under pressure and speed up the spawn of dots if they are doing well.

Remember that you used an after call inside the **add_dot** function to schedule another dot in 1000 milliseconds (or 1 second)? Go back and find that line – you're going to change it a bit.

First, create a variable speed and set it to 1000. Then, instead of scheduling a call to add a dot after 1000 ms, schedule it to add a dot after speed milliseconds. This will have absolutely no effect on the game... yet. You are still scheduling the next call after 1000 ms, but that figure is now coming from the variable speed instead of being hard-coded as a magic number.

```
speed = 1000
board.after(speed, add_dot)
```

Now here's how you can ramp up the pressure. Between these two lines of code, you can add some code to set the speed of dots depending on the current score. Here is an example:

```
speed = 1000
if score > 10:
    speed = 500
elif score > 20:
    speed = 400
elif score > 30:
    speed = 200
board.after(speed, add_dot)
```

Here, you can see that if the player has got more than 10 points, the new dots will appear every 500ms, if they have more than 20 points a dot will appear every 400ms, and so on. This makes the game much harder the more points you have. Save your code – **destroy6.py** – and test the game to see the difference. You can alter the numbers or add more `elif` conditions if you want to increase the difficulty even further.

Game over

All that remains is to figure out when the player has lost the game; this happens when every square has turned into a red dot.

Remember that when you made Tic-tac-toe, you used *nested loops* to check whether all squares were filled and the game was a draw? You can use the same method here too, to loop through every square on the grid and check if it is a red dot. In your **add_dot** function, just before the call to **after**, add some code for a nested loop to loop through all squares on the board:

```
all_red = True
for x in range(GRID_SIZE):
    for y in range(GRID_SIZE):
```

The first line begins by assuming that all squares are red. The nested loop will provide the coordinates of every square on the grid in turn, as the values **x** and **y** so that you can check whether this is true.

Add some code inside the second loop to find out whether the current pixel is red, and if it is *not*, change the **all_red** variable to False.

```
all_red = True
for x in range(GRID_SIZE):
    for y in range(GRID_SIZE):
        if board[x,y].color != "red":
            all_red = False
```

Chapter 7 Destroy the Dots

After both loops end (make sure you unindent the following code), check whether the grid was all red dots. If it is, the player has lost so display a message:

```
if all_red:
    score_display.value = "You lost! Score: " + str(score)
```

If the player hasn't lost, the game should continue. Add an `else:` and inside it, indent the `after` method you already have, as we only want to add a new dot if the player has *not* lost:

```
else:
    board.after(speed, add_dot)
```

Be careful to indent the `after` line you already have here rather than adding another one, or your game will start behaving strangely and generate multiple dots per second!

Your final code should resemble **07-destroy-the-dots.py**. Enjoy the game.

USING CONSTANTS

Setting the height and width of your Waffle to 5 is known as using a 'magic number' in a program, because the specific number is hard-coded into the program. If you want to change the size of the grid, you will need to find everywhere in the program this number appears and change it, which might be messy.

Better programming practice would be to define a *constant* in your variables section called **GRID_SIZE** and set it equal to 5:

GRID_SIZE = 5

Then, instead of defining your Waffle's dimensions with a magic number 5, you can put:

board = Waffle(app, width=GRID_SIZE, height=GRID_SIZE)

If you decide to change the size of the grid, you can just change the value of this constant.

Thinking about this type of thing at the time you write the program will help you to avoid headaches later if you decide to change it.

CHALLENGE

- Can you add a reset button which allows the player to begin a new game without having to rerun the program?
- Can you put even more pressure on the player by calculating how many red dots are on the board, and increasing the speed in proportion to the number of red dots?

destroy1.py / Python 3

```python
# Imports --------------

from guizero import App, Text, Waffle


# Variables ------------


# Functions ------------


# App ------------------

app = App("Destroy the dots")

instructions = Text(app, text="Click the dots to destroy them")
board = Waffle(app, width=5, height=5)

app.display()
```

DOWNLOAD
magpi.cc/guizerocode

destroy2.py / Python 3

```python
# Imports --------------

from guizero import App, Text, Waffle
from random import randint


# Variables ------------

GRID_SIZE = 5


# Functions ------------

def add_dot():
    x, y = randint(0,GRID_SIZE-1), randint(0,GRID_SIZE-1)
    while board[x, y].dotty == True:
        x, y = randint(0,GRID_SIZE-1), randint(0,GRID_SIZE-1)
    board[x, y].dotty = True
```

destroy2.py (cont.) / Python 3

```python
        board.set_pixel(x, y, "red")


# App ------------------

app = App("Destroy the dots")

instructions = Text(app, text="Click the dots to destroy them")
board = Waffle(app, width=5, height=5)
add_dot()

app.display()
```

destroy3.py / Python 3

```python
# Imports ---------------

from guizero import App, Text, Waffle
from random import randint


# Variables -------------

GRID_SIZE = 5


# Functions -------------

def add_dot():
    x, y = randint(0,GRID_SIZE-1), randint(0,GRID_SIZE-1)
    while board[x, y].dotty == True:
        x, y = randint(0,GRID_SIZE-1), randint(0,GRID_SIZE-1)
    board[x, y].dotty = True
    board.set_pixel(x, y, "red")

def destroy_dot(x, y):
    if board[x,y].dotty == True:
        board[x,y].dotty = False
        board.set_pixel(x, y, "white")
```

CREATE GRAPHICAL USER INTERFACES WITH PYTHON

destroy3.py (cont.) / Python 3

```python
# App ------------------

app = App("Destroy the dots")

instructions = Text(app, text="Click the dots to destroy them")
board = Waffle(app, width=GRID_SIZE, height=GRID_SIZE,
command=destroy_dot)
add_dot()

app.display()
```

destroy4.py / Python 3

```python
# Imports --------------

from guizero import App, Text, Waffle
from random import randint

# Variables ------------

GRID_SIZE = 5

# Functions ------------

def add_dot():
    x, y = randint(0,GRID_SIZE-1), randint(0,GRID_SIZE-1)
    while board[x, y].dotty == True:
        x, y = randint(0,GRID_SIZE-1), randint(0,GRID_SIZE-1)
    board[x, y].dotty = True
    board.set_pixel(x, y, "red")
    board.after(1000, add_dot)

def destroy_dot(x,y):
    if board[x,y].dotty == True:
        board[x,y].dotty = False
        board.set_pixel(x, y, "white")

# App ------------------
```

Chapter 7 Destroy the Dots

destroy4.py (cont.) / Python 3

```python
app = App("Destroy the dots")

instructions = Text(app, text="Click the dots to destroy them")
board = Waffle(app, width=GRID_SIZE, height=GRID_SIZE,
command=destroy_dot)
board.after(1000, add_dot)

app.display()
```

destroy5.py / Python 3

```python
# Imports --------------

from guizero import App, Text, Waffle
from random import randint

# Variables -------------

GRID_SIZE = 5
score = 0

# Functions -------------

def add_dot():
    x, y = randint(0,GRID_SIZE-1), randint(0,GRID_SIZE-1)
    while board[x, y].dotty == True:
        x, y = randint(0,GRID_SIZE-1), randint(0,GRID_SIZE-1)
    board[x, y].dotty = True
    board.set_pixel(x, y, "red")
    board.after(1000, add_dot)

def destroy_dot(x,y):
    global score
    if board[x,y].dotty == True:
        board[x,y].dotty = False
        board.set_pixel(x, y, "white")
        score += 1
        score_display.value = "Your score is " + str(score)
```

destroy5.py (cont.) / Python 3

```
# App -------------------

app = App("Destroy the dots")

instructions = Text(app, text="Click the dots to destroy them")
board = Waffle(app, width=GRID_SIZE, height=GRID_SIZE,
command=destroy_dot)
board.after(1000, add_dot)
score_display = Text(app, text="Your score is " + str(score))

app.display()
```

destroy6.py / Python 3

```
# Imports ---------------

from guizero import App, Text, Waffle
from random import randint

# Variables -------------

GRID_SIZE = 5
score = 0

# Functions -------------

def add_dot():
    x, y = randint(0,GRID_SIZE-1), randint(0,GRID_SIZE-1)
    while board[x, y].dotty == True:
        x, y = randint(0,GRID_SIZE-1), randint(0,GRID_SIZE-1)
    board[x, y].dotty = True
    board.set_pixel(x, y, "red")

    speed = 1000
    if score > 10:
        speed = 500
    elif score > 20:
        speed = 400
    elif score > 30:
```

destroy6.py (cont.) / Python 3

```python
        speed = 200
    board.after(speed, add_dot)

def destroy_dot(x,y):
    global score
    if board[x,y].dotty == True:
        board[x,y].dotty = False
        board.set_pixel(x, y, "white")
        score += 1
        score_display.value = "Your score is " + str(score)


# App -------------------

app = App("Destroy the dots")

instructions = Text(app, text="Click the dots to destroy them")
board = Waffle(app, width=GRID_SIZE, height=GRID_SIZE,
command=destroy_dot)
board.after(1000, add_dot)
score_display = Text(app, text="Your score is " + str(score))

app.display()
```

07-destroy-the-dots.py / Python 3

```python
# Imports ---------------

from guizero import App, Text, Waffle
from random import randint

# Variables -------------

GRID_SIZE = 5
score = 0

# Functions -------------

def add_dot():
    x, y = randint(0,GRID_SIZE-1), randint(0,GRID_SIZE-1)
    while board[x, y].dotty == True:
```

07-destroy-the-dots.py (cont.) / Python 3

```python
        x, y = randint(0,GRID_SIZE-1), randint(0,GRID_SIZE-1)
    board[x, y].dotty = True
    board.set_pixel(x, y, "red")

    speed = 1000
    if score > 10:
        speed = 500
    elif score > 20:
        speed = 400
    elif score > 30:
        speed = 200

    all_red = True
    for x in range(GRID_SIZE):
        for y in range(GRID_SIZE):
            if board[x,y].color != "red":
                all_red = False
    if all_red:
        score_display.value = "You lost! Score: " + str(score)
    else:
        board.after(speed, add_dot)

def destroy_dot(x,y):
    global score
    if board[x,y].dotty == True:
        board[x,y].dotty = False
        board.set_pixel(x, y, "white")
        score += 1
        score_display.value = "Your score is " + str(score)

# App -------------------

app = App("Destroy the dots")

instructions = Text(app, text="Click the dots to destroy them")
board = Waffle(app, width=GRID_SIZE, height=GRID_SIZE, command=destroy_dot)
board.after(1000, add_dot)
score_display = Text(app, text="Your score is " + str(score))

app.display()
```

Chapter 8
Flood It

Create a more complex Waffle-based puzzle game

'Flood It' is a game where the aim is to flood the board with all squares the same colour. Beginning with the top-left square, players choose a colour to flood into. It offers a slightly more complex Waffle-based game.

Aim of the game

In this example (**Figure 1**), the top-left square is yellow. The player could either choose to flood into the single blue square to the right, or to flood into the red square underneath.

Flooding the red square would be a better move because all adjoining red squares would also be flooded, and the player is only allowed a limited amount of moves before the game ends.

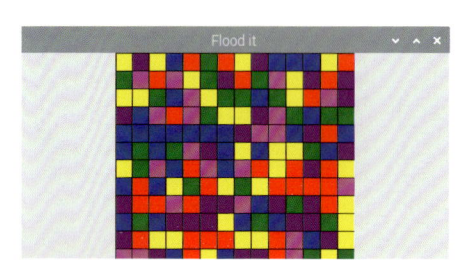

▲ **Figure 1** Flood the squares with one colour

Set up

Download (from **magpi.cc/floodit**) and open the starter file, **floodit_starter.py**. Save it in a sensible place.

In the variables section, give the variables some values:

- `colours` – a list of six colours as strings. These can either be common colour names or hex colours. The colour names "white", "black", "red", "green", "blue", "cyan", "yellow", and "magenta" will always be available.
- `board_size` – the width/height of the board as an integer; we chose 14. The board is always a square.
- `moves_limit` – how many moves the player is allowed before they lose, as an integer; we chose 25.

In the app section, create an App widget and give it a title.

```
app = App("Flood it")
app.display()
```

Running this will result in a standard labelled window (**Figure 2**).

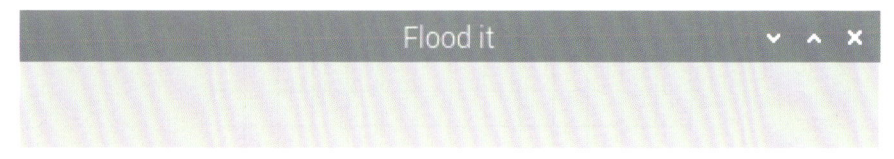

🔺 **Figure 2** The usual labelled window

Create the board

The board is a grid of squares, each containing a randomly selected colour from the list you created earlier.

Inside the app, add a Waffle widget. This will create a grid which will be the board.

```
board = Waffle(app)
```

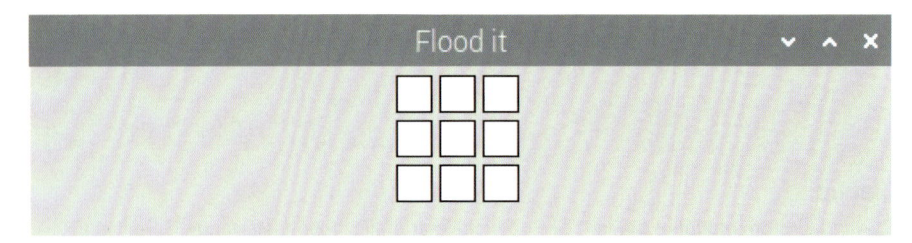

▲ **Figure 3** The grid squares are too small

Run your program and you will see that the grid is a bit too small (**Figure 3**).

Add to the line of code you just wrote to specify parameters for the width and height of the Waffle, and make the padding between the grid squares zero.

```
board = Waffle(app, width=board_size, height=board_size, pad=0)
```

That's better (**Figure 4**).

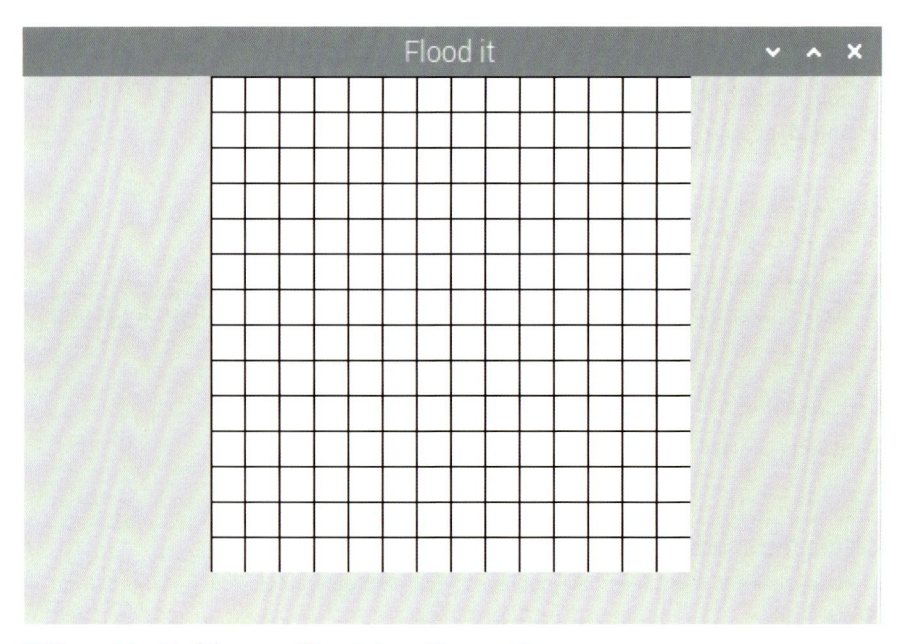

▲ **Figure 4** A grid of the correct board size, with no padding

CREATE GRAPHICAL USER INTERFACES WITH PYTHON

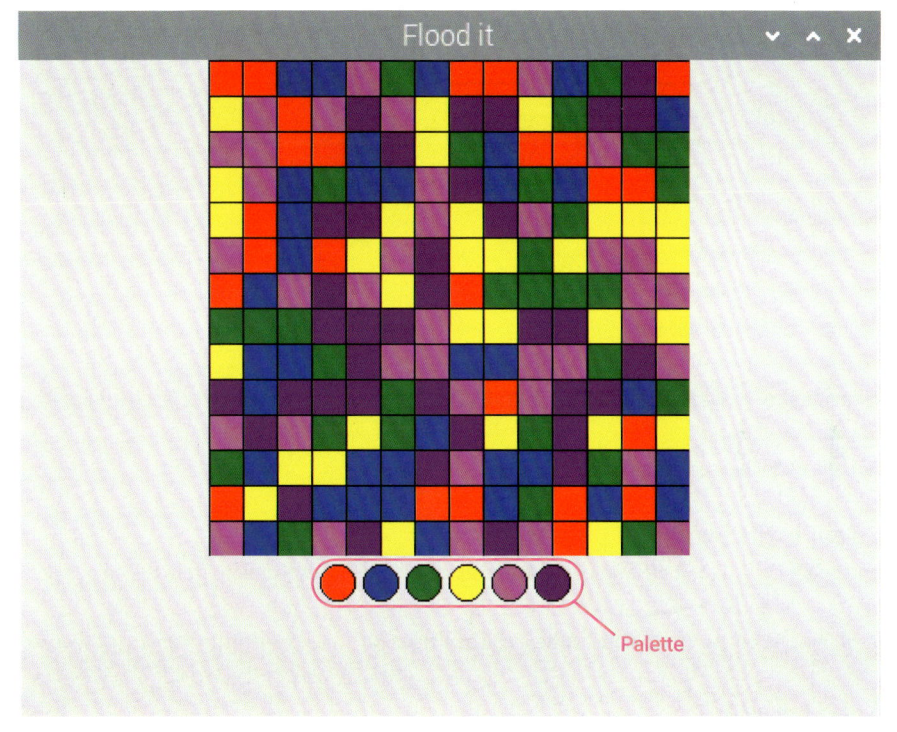

▲ **Figure 5** You'll need a palette for the player to choose a colour

Create the palette

The palette shows the player which colours they can click on to flood the board. They will click on these colours to play the game. The palette from the finished game is shown in **Figure 5**.

On the line after you created the board, create another Waffle, but this time it should be called `palette`.

```
palette = Waffle(app)
```

Remember when you added the parameters to the board Waffle in the previous step? This time, add these parameters to the `palette` Waffle with each one separated by a comma:

`width = 6` (the number of colours we have)
`height = 1`
`dotty = True` (this makes the squares into circles)

Chapter 8 Flood it   81

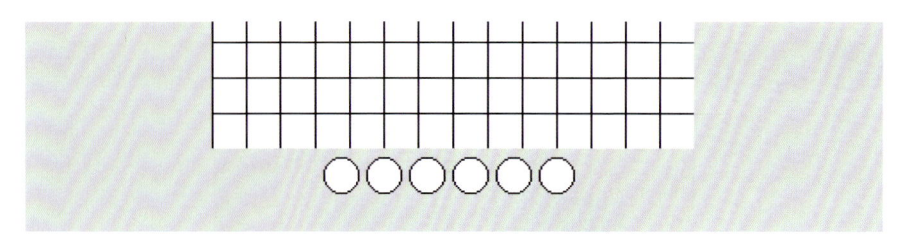

▲ **Figure 6** A blank palette

So, now you should have:

```
palette = Waffle(app, width=6, height=1, dotty=True)
```

Run the code to see a blank palette (**Figure 6**).

Colour in the board

The board should start off with each square as a randomly chosen colour from the colours list you created earlier.

On the line below your palette, write a call to a function

```
fill_board()
```

Find the functions section in your program, and begin writing the code for this new function:

```
def fill_board():
```

You can write a nested loop to loop through every row and column in the board. Each pixel will be coloured with a randomly chosen colour from the list. To colour in a pixel, you will use this code, where the **?** symbols will be replaced with the x, y co-ordinates of the pixel:

```
board.set_pixel(?, ?, random.choice(colours))
```

Try to write the code yourself using what you have learnt about nested loops in the previous chapters – the solution is provided on page 83 if you get stuck.

Hint: Use the `board_size` variable to know how many times to loop.

When you run your code, you should see a colourful board. If you see a white board, double-check that you put in the function call to `fill_board()` (**Figure 7**).

CREATE GRAPHICAL USER INTERFACES WITH PYTHON

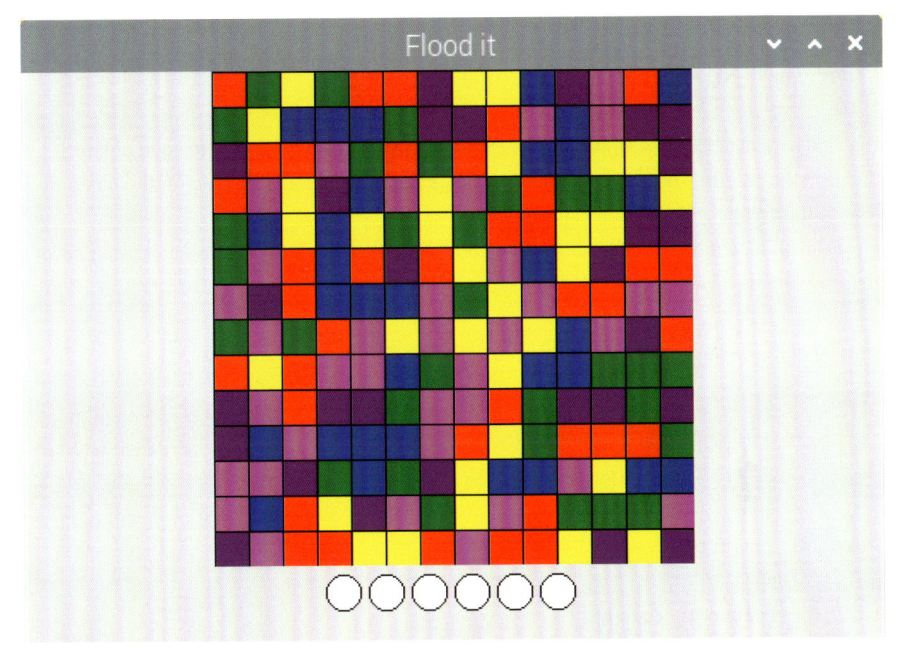

Figure 7 Each square of the board is coloured randomly

Here is one solution, but there are many ways you could do this:

```
def fill_board():
    for x in range(board_size):
        for y in range(board_size):
            board.set_pixel(x, y, random.choice(colours))
```

An alternative solution which uses a more advanced feature called a list comprehension:

```
def fill_board():
    [board.set_pixel(x, y, random.choice(colours)) for y in range(board_size) for x in range(board_size)]
```

Colour in the palette

Now that you have a colourful board, let's colour in the palette.

On the line below your `fill_board()` code, write a call to a function:

```
init_palette()
```

Find the functions section in your program, and begin writing the code for this new function:

```
def init_palette():
```

The idea here is to loop through all of the colours in the list, assigning one to each of the circles in the palette. You can use the same `set_pixel` method as you used for the board to change the colour of the circles in the palette.

Have a go at writing the code yourself. If you get stuck, some possible solutions are shown in the 'How many ways can you colour the palette' box.

Hint: *All of the circles in the palette are in row 0 of the Waffle.*

HOW MANY WAYS CAN YOU COLOUR THE PALETTE?

Here is a solution which uses a loop and a variable to keep track of which column you are colouring in:

```
def init_palette():
    column = 0
    for colour in colours:
        palette.set_pixel(column, 0, colour)
        column += 1
```

Here is a similar solution which uses a range inside the `for` loop instead of a counter variable:

```
def init_palette():
    for x in range(len(colours)):
        palette.set_pixel(x, 0, colours[x])
```

Here is a different solution which uses the index function `colours.index(colour)`. This code says 'In the colours list, find me the position in the list of colour'. So, for example if your list was `["green", "blue", "red"]` then the index of green would be 0, the index of blue would be 1, etc., remembering that we count starting from zero.

```
def init_palette():
    for colour in colours:
        palette.set_pixel(colours.index(colour), 0, colour)
```

You can use any of these solutions, or you may have come up with a different way by yourself. None of them is the 'right answer': there are often many different ways of coding a solution.

Start the flood

When the player clicks on a colour in the palette, the board should flood with that colour, beginning with the top-left square.

In the functions section, create a new function called **start_flood** in exactly the same way as you did for the last two functions. This function needs to take two parameters which will be the x, y co-ordinates of the square that was clicked on. Add these between the brackets so that you end up with your code looking like this:

```
def start_flood(x, y):
```

Add a line of code (indented) to the function get the name of the colour that was clicked on:

```
flood_colour = palette.get_pixel(x,y)
```

This will be the colour to flood the board with.

Add a line of code to get the current colour of the starting pixel – this is always the pixel in the top left of the board, at co-ordinates 0, 0.

```
target = board.get_pixel(0,0)
```

Now call the **flood** function, which has already been written for you in the starter file. This function starts at 0,0 and floods all the pixels connected to the top-left pixel that are the same colour with the **flood_colour**.

```
flood(0, 0, target, flood_colour)
```

This function should run whenever someone clicks on a colour in the palette, so find the line of code where you created the palette.

```
palette = Waffle(app, width=6, height=1, dotty=True)
```

Add another parameter which is a command. When a circle on the palette is clicked, this command will be executed. The command is the function **start_flood**, so your code should now look like this:

```
palette = Waffle(app, width=6, height=1, dotty=True,
command=start_flood)
```

Test out your code by clicking on the circles on the palette.

The top-left square is green (**Figure 8**). If you click red on the palette, the top-left square will turn red and connect to the other red squares (**Figure 9**).

Now there are four red squares connected to the top-left square. Let's click green to connect up the green squares underneath (**Figure 10**).

Now there is a large chain of green squares. Continue the game by pressing different colours in the palette. The aim is to eventually get all of the squares the same colour.

Winning the game

At the moment, if the player manages to get all of the squares in the grid the same colour, nothing happens. The player is also allowed an infinite number of turns, as the number of moves they have taken is not tracked.

First let's add a piece of text to the GUI to display whether the player has won or lost. The text will start off blank.

Underneath the code for the palette, add a Text widget called `win_text`.

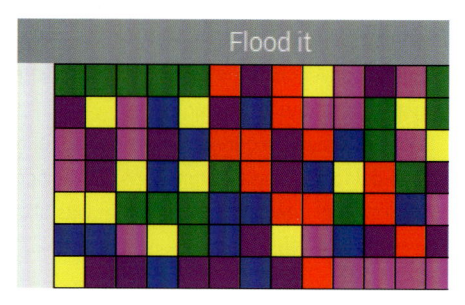

▲ **Figure 8** Here, the top-left square is green

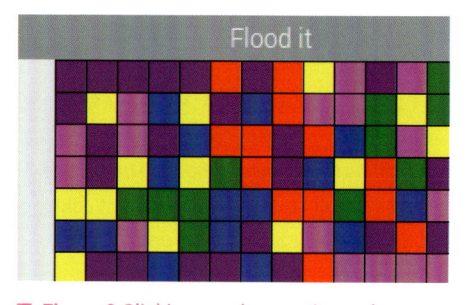

▲ **Figure 9** Clicking purple turns it purple

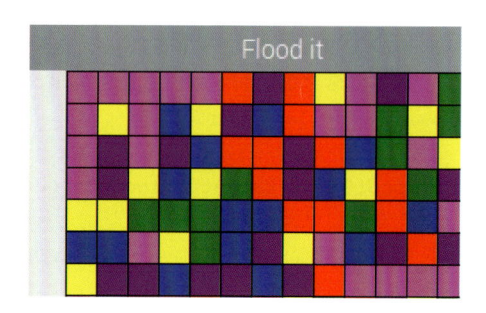

▲ **Figure 10** Click pink for a chain of pink

```
win_text = Text(app)
```

In the variables section, add another variable called `moves_taken` and set it to 0.

Now create a function called `win_check` to check after each move whether the player has won.

First, you need to specify that you would like to be allowed to change the value of the global variable `moves_taken`.

```
global moves_taken
```

Then add 1 to the `moves_taken` variable – each time this function is called, we will add one more move.

```
moves_taken += 1
```

Check if the `moves_taken` is less than the `moves_limit` or not:

```
if moves_taken < moves_limit:
```

```
else:
```

If the `moves_taken` is not within the limit, this means the playher has run out of moves, so update the text to say that they lost:

```
if moves_taken < moves_limit:

else:
    win_text.value = "You lost :("
```

If the number of moves taken *is* less than the limit, check whether all of the squares are the same colour by calling the function already written for you in the starter file. Make sure the following code is indented below the first `if` statement:

```
if all_squares_are_the_same():
    win_text.value = "You win!"
```

The completed piece of code should look like this:

```
def win_check():
    moves_taken += 1
    if moves_taken <= moves_limit:
        if all_squares_are_the_same():
            win_text.value = "You win!"
    else:
        win_text.value = "You lost :("
```

Finally, you must call the `win_check` function whenever a square is clicked on. The easiest way to do this is to add the function call at the end of the `start_flood` function.

Now it's time to test the game. An example code listing is shown in **08-floodit.py**, overleaf.

Test your game

You can test whether the game works by playing it; however, it might take a long time to test whether you can win! An easier way to check is to change the `board_size` variable to something small such as 5, and then play the game on a much smaller grid to see whether you can win.

You can easily test whether the game causes you to lose properly by clicking on the same colour 25 times!

> **CHALLENGE**
>
> - If the player wins or the player loses, disable the palette to prevent them clicking on it any more and causing an error. The code to disable the palette is `palette.disable()`.
>
> - Display how many moves are left as a piece of text on the GUI.
>
> - Add a button which displays instructions for how to play.
>
> - Add a reset button to let the player start a new game. Don't forget, you will also have to reset the colours on the board, reset the `moves_taken` variable, and re-enable the palette if you disabled it (`palette.enable()`).

08-floodit.py / Python 3

DOWNLOAD
magpi.cc/guizerocode

```python
# -----------------------------
# Imports
# -----------------------------

from guizero import App, Waffle, Text, PushButton, info
import random

# -----------------------------
# Variables
# -----------------------------

colours = ["red", "blue", "green", "yellow", "magenta", "purple"]
board_size = 14
moves_limit = 25
moves_taken = 0

# -----------------------------
# Functions
# -----------------------------

# Recursively floods adjacent squares
def flood(x, y, target, replacement):
    # Algorithm from https://en.wikipedia.org/wiki/Flood_fill
    if target == replacement:
        return False
    if board.get_pixel(x, y) != target:
        return False
    board.set_pixel(x, y, replacement)
    if y+1 <= board_size-1:    # South
        flood(x, y+1, target, replacement)
    if y-1 >= 0:               # North
        flood(x, y-1, target, replacement)
    if x+1 <= board_size-1:    # East
        flood(x+1, y, target, replacement)
    if x-1 >= 0:               # West
        flood(x-1, y, target, replacement)

# Check whether all squares are the same
def all_squares_are_the_same():
    squares = board.get_all()
    if all(colour == squares[0] for colour in squares):
        return True
```

08-floodit.py (cont.) / Python 3

```python
    else:
        return False

def win_check():
    global moves_taken
    moves_taken += 1
    if moves_taken <= moves_limit:
        if all_squares_are_the_same():
            win_text.value = "You win!"
    else:
        win_text.value = "You lost :("

def fill_board():
    for x in range(board_size):
        for y in range(board_size):
            board.set_pixel(x, y, random.choice(colours))

def init_palette():
    for colour in colours:
        palette.set_pixel(colours.index(colour), 0, colour)

def start_flood(x, y):
    flood_colour = palette.get_pixel(x,y)
    target = board.get_pixel(0,0)
    flood(0, 0, target, flood_colour)
    win_check()

# -------------------------------
# App
# -------------------------------

app = App("Flood it")

board = Waffle(app, width=board_size, height=board_size, pad=0)
palette = Waffle(app, width=6, height=1, dotty=True,
command=start_flood)

win_text = Text(app)

fill_board()
init_palette()

app.display()
```

Chapter 9
Emoji Match
Create a fun picture-matching game

You are going to build an emoji picture-matching game (Figure 1). The object of the game is to spot the one emoji that appears in two different sets. You get a point for each correct match and lose a point for an incorrect match.

Loading emojis
To create the game, you will need emojis. You can use the emojis created for Twitter (**twemoji.twitter.com**). Download the **emojis.zip** file from **magpi.cc/guizeroemojis**, open the zip file, and copy the **emojis** folder to the folder where you save your code.

The game will need to choose nine emojis at random and arrange them into a grid. A simple way to do this is to put all of the emojis into a list and randomly shuffle them.

The following code creates a shuffled list of items, each in the form **path/emoji_file_name**.

Create a new program with the usual commented lines for different sections (Imports, Variables, Functions, App). Under imports, add:

```
import os
from random import shuffle
```

Then, under variables, enter this code which creates a shuffled list of emojis, each in the form **path/emoji_file_name**.

```
# set the path to the emoji folder on your computer
emojis_dir = "emojis"
emojis = [os.path.join(emojis_dir, f) for f in os.listdir(emojis_dir)]
shuffle(emojis)
```

The `emojis_dir` variable is the path of the emojis on your computer; it will tell the code that loads the emojis where to find them.

Test your program. Try printing the `emojis` list to the screen with `print(emojis)`. You should see a long list of file names. The list should be in a different order each time you run it.

Displaying the emojis

Next, the code needs to create two 3×3 grids of Picture and PushButton widgets which will show the emojis.

Modify your program to create a guizero app and a Box to hold the picture widgets using a `"grid"` layout. In the imports section, add this line to import the required widgets:

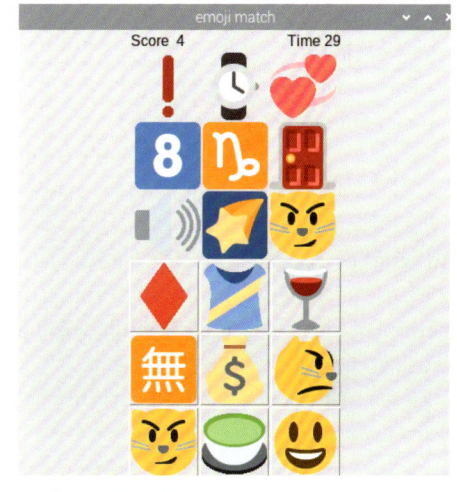

🔺 **Figure 1** The finished game

```
from guizero import App, Box
```

In the app section, add the following code:

```
app = App("emoji match")

pictures_box = Box(app, layout="grid")
```

The Box widget is really useful for laying out your GUI. It's an invisible area of your GUI where you can group widgets together. A Box can have its own layout, size, and bg (background). They can also be hidden or shown, meaning you can easily make a collection of widgets invisible.

If you wish to *see* the Box, you can add a border by setting the parameter to True.

```
pictures_box = Box(app, layout="grid", border=True)
```

Now, add the Picture widget to your imports:

```
from guizero import App, Box, Picture
```

In the app section, add in the code to create the Picture widgets and add them to a list.

```
pictures = []

for x in range(0,3):
    for y in range(0,3):
        picture = Picture(pictures_box, grid=[x,y])
        pictures.append(picture)
```

To assign co-ordinates to each Picture widget, two **for** loops are used. They both run through the range 0–2; one assigns its value to the variable **x** and the other to the variable **y**. The grid position of each widget is set using the **x** and **y** values. The widgets are appended to a list so they can be referenced later in the game.

Do the same for PushButton widgets to create the second 3×3 grid. First, add the widget to your imports:

```
from guizero import App, Box, Picture, PushButton
```

In the app section, add lines so it looks like this:

```
app = App("emoji match")

pictures_box = Box(app, layout="grid")
buttons_box = Box(app, layout="grid")

pictures = []
buttons = []

for x in range(0,3):
    for y in range(0,3):
```

```
        picture = Picture(pictures_box, grid=[x,y])
        pictures.append(picture)

        button = PushButton(buttons_box, grid=[x,y])
        buttons.append(button)
```

In the functions section, create a function to set up each round of the game.

```
def setup_round():
    for picture in pictures:
        picture.image = emojis.pop()

    for button in buttons:
        button.image = emojis.pop()
```

To assign each `picture` and `button` widget an emoji, the `image` property is set to an item from the `emojis` list. Emojis are selected using `pop()`, which chooses the last item in a list and then removes it from the list. I've used this function because it will prevent any emoji appearing in the game more than once.

At the bottom of your program, call the `setup_round` function and display the app.

```
setup_round()

app.display()
```

Your program should now resemble **emoji1.py** (page 99). Test it and you should see two grids of nine emojis.

Matching emojis

At the moment, all of the emojis in your app will be different (**Figure 2**). In the next step, you will pick another emoji to match, and update one picture and one button so they have the same matching emoji.

Add `randint` to your `random` import line. This is used to obtain a number from 0 to 8 for each picture and button.

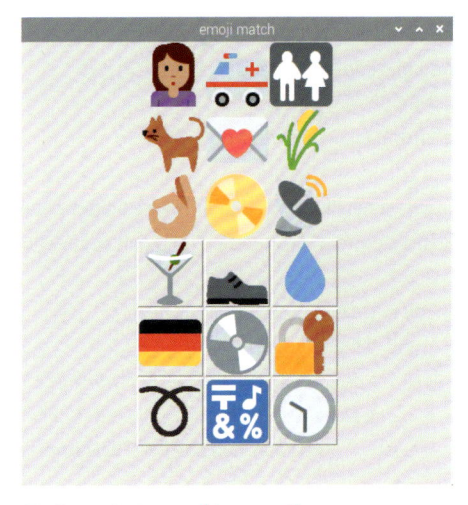

▲ **Figure 2** No matching emojis

```
from random import shuffle, randint
```

Then add this code (indented) to the bottom of the `setup_round` function to pop another emoji from the list and set it to be the image of a random picture and button.

```
matched_emoji = emojis.pop()

random_picture = randint(0,8)
pictures[random_picture].image = matched_emoji

random_button = randint(0,8)
buttons[random_button].image = matched_emoji
```

Your code should now look like **emoji2.py**. Run your program now; one of the emojis should match. Look carefully – the matching emoji can be hard to spot.

Check the guess

Each time one of the PushButtons is pressed, it will need to check if this is the matching emoji and put the result 'correct' or 'incorrect' on the screen. After the player's guess, a new round will be set up and different set of emojis displayed.

Your app will need a Text widget display the result. Add it to your imports:

```
from guizero import App, Box, Picture, PushButton, Text
```

Add this line in your app section:

```
result = Text(app)
```

Create a new function which will be called when one of the emoji buttons is pressed. It will display 'correct' or 'incorrect' and call `setup_round` to create the next set of emojis.

```
def match_emoji(matched):
    if matched:
        result.value = "correct"
    else:
        result.value = "incorrect"

    setup_round()
```

The incorrect emoji buttons will pass False to the `match_emoji` function; the matching emoji will pass True.

Update the `setup_round` function so that all the 'incorrect' buttons call the `match_emoji` function.

```
for button in buttons:
    button.image = emojis.pop()
    button.update_command(match_emoji, args=[False])
```

The `update_command` method sets the function which will be called when the button is pressed. The `args` list `[False]` will be used as the parameters to the `match_emoji` function.

Finally, update the command for the matching button so it calls `match_emoji`, but this time passes True as the argument.

```
buttons[random_button].update_command(match_emoji, [True])
```

Your code should now resemble **emoji3.py**. Play the game. In each round there will be a matching emoji – press the matching picture button. Did you get it right?

Adding a score and timer

At the moment, the game continues forever (or until you run out of emojis in the list). Add a score and a timer which counts down to the end of the game to give a challenge.

In the app section, create two Text widgets to show the score and the timer.

```
score = Text(app, text="0")
timer = Text(app, text="30")
```

The timer is set to `"30"`, which will be the number of seconds in each round.

Modify the `match_emoji` function to either add or subtract 1 to/from the player's score.

```
def match_emoji(matched):
    if matched:
        result.value = "correct"
        score.value = int(score.value) + 1
    else:
        result.value = "incorrect"
        score.value = int(score.value) - 1
```

To create the timer, you will use a feature of guizero which allows you to ask the application to continuously call a function every 1 second.

Create a function which will reduce the value of the timer by 1.

```
def reduce_time():
    timer.value = int(timer.value) - 1
```

Before the app is displayed, use the `app.repeat()` function to call the `reduce_time` function every second (1000 milliseconds).

```
app.repeat(1000, reduce_time)
```

```
app.display()
```

Running your game now, you will notice that the timer counts down from 30. Unfortunately, it will continue counting down past 0 and never stop.

Update the `reduce_time` function to check if the timer is less than zero and then stop the game.

```
def reduce_time():
    timer.value = int(timer.value) - 1
    # is it game over?
    if int(timer.value) < 0:
        result.value = "Game over! Score = " + score.value
        # hide the game
        pictures_box.hide()
        buttons_box.hide()
        timer.hide()
        score.hide()
```

When the timer is less than 0, the message 'game over' is displayed and the game's widgets are hidden so the user can no longer play.

See **emoji4.py** to get an idea of how your code should now look. Run it and play the emoji match game. Challenge a friend or family member to a game.

You may want to put the score and timer widgets into a Box so they can be laid out better (**Figure 3**) – see the complete **09-emoji-match.py** listing for how to do this.

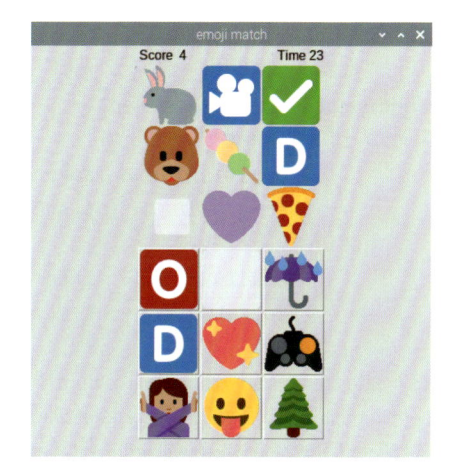

▲ **Figure 3** With box for score and timer

CREATE GRAPHICAL USER INTERFACES WITH PYTHON

CHALLENGE

At the moment, the only way to start a new round of the game is restart the program. Can you change the code to introduce a button to start a new round?

USING OTHER IMAGES

The emoji match game uses picture buttons to allow the user to pick which emoji matches. You can make any PushButton widget into a picture button by setting the image parameter; for example:

```
button = PushButton(app, image="my_picture.gif")
```

The button will scale to fit the size of your image. The type of image you can use is determined by your operating system and how you installed guizero, although any setup will support GIF images. To find the image file types supported by your setup, you can run:

```
from guizero import system_config
print(system_config.supported_image_types)
```

You can find out more about image support in guizero at **lawsie.github.io/guizero/images**.

emoji1.py / Python 3

⬇ **DOWNLOAD**

magpi.cc/guizerocode

```python
# -------------------------------
# Imports
# -------------------------------

import os
from random import shuffle
from guizero import App, Box, Picture, PushButton


# -------------------------------
# Variables
# -------------------------------

# set the path to the emoji folder on your computer
emojis_dir = "emojis"
```

emoji1.py (cont.) / Python 3

```python
emojis = [os.path.join(emojis_dir, f) for f in os.listdir(emojis_dir)]
shuffle(emojis)


# ------------------------------
# Functions
# ------------------------------

def setup_round():
    for picture in pictures:
        picture.image = emojis.pop()

    for button in buttons:
        button.image = emojis.pop()


# ------------------------------
# App
# ------------------------------

app = App("emoji match")

pictures_box = Box(app, layout="grid")
buttons_box = Box(app, layout="grid")

pictures = []
buttons = []

for x in range(0,3):
    for y in range(0,3):
        picture = Picture(pictures_box, grid=[x,y])
        pictures.append(picture)

        button = PushButton(buttons_box, grid=[x,y])
        buttons.append(button)

setup_round()

app.display()
```

emoji2.py / Python 3

```python
# -----------------------------
# Imports
# -----------------------------

import os
from random import shuffle, randint
from guizero import App, Box, Picture, PushButton


# -----------------------------
# Variables
# -----------------------------

# set the path to the emoji folder on your computer
emojis_dir = "emojis"
emojis = [os.path.join(emojis_dir, f) for f in os.listdir(emojis_dir)]
shuffle(emojis)


# -----------------------------
# Functions
# -----------------------------

def setup_round():
    for picture in pictures:
        picture.image = emojis.pop()

    for button in buttons:
        button.image = emojis.pop()

    matched_emoji = emojis.pop()

    random_picture = randint(0,8)
    pictures[random_picture].image = matched_emoji

    random_button = randint(0,8)
    buttons[random_button].image = matched_emoji
```

emoji2.py (cont.) / Python 3

```python
# -------------------------------
# App
# -------------------------------

app = App("emoji match")

pictures_box = Box(app, layout="grid")
buttons_box = Box(app, layout="grid")

pictures = []
buttons = []

for x in range(0,3):
    for y in range(0,3):
        picture = Picture(pictures_box, grid=[x,y])
        pictures.append(picture)

        button = PushButton(buttons_box, grid=[x,y])
        buttons.append(button)

setup_round()

app.display()
```

emoji3.py / Python 3

```python
# -------------------------------
# Imports
# -------------------------------

import os
from random import shuffle, randint
from guizero import App, Box, Picture, PushButton, Text


# -------------------------------
# Variables
# -------------------------------

# set the path to the emoji folder on your computer
```

emoji3.py (cont.) / Python 3

```python
emojis_dir = "emojis"
emojis = [os.path.join(emojis_dir, f) for f in os.listdir(emojis_dir)]
shuffle(emojis)


# -----------------------------
# Functions
# -----------------------------

def setup_round():
    for picture in pictures:
        picture.image = emojis.pop()

    for button in buttons:
        button.image = emojis.pop()
        button.update_command(match_emoji, args=[False])

    matched_emoji = emojis.pop()

    random_picture = randint(0,8)
    pictures[random_picture].image = matched_emoji

    random_button = randint(0,8)
    buttons[random_button].image = matched_emoji

    buttons[random_button].update_command(match_emoji, [True])

def match_emoji(matched):
    if matched:
        result.value = "correct"
    else:
        result.value = "incorrect"

    setup_round()


# -----------------------------
# App
# -----------------------------
```

emoji3.py (cont.) / Python 3

```python
app = App("emoji match")

pictures_box = Box(app, layout="grid")
buttons_box = Box(app, layout="grid")

pictures = []
buttons = []

for x in range(0,3):
    for y in range(0,3):
        picture = Picture(pictures_box, grid=[x,y])
        pictures.append(picture)

        button = PushButton(buttons_box, grid=[x,y])
        buttons.append(button)

result = Text(app)

setup_round()

app.display()
```

emoji4.py / Python 3

```python
# -------------------------------
# Imports
# -------------------------------

import os
from random import shuffle, randint
from guizero import App, Box, Picture, PushButton, Text


# -------------------------------
# Variables
# -------------------------------

# set the path to the emoji folder on your computer
emojis_dir = "emojis"
emojis = [os.path.join(emojis_dir, f) for f in os.listdir(emojis_
```

emoji4.py (cont.) / Python 3

```python
dir)]
shuffle(emojis)


# -----------------------------
# Functions
# -----------------------------

def setup_round():
    for picture in pictures:
        picture.image = emojis.pop()

    for button in buttons:
        button.image = emojis.pop()
        button.update_command(match_emoji, args=[False])

    matched_emoji = emojis.pop()

    random_picture = randint(0,8)
    pictures[random_picture].image = matched_emoji

    random_button = randint(0,8)
    buttons[random_button].image = matched_emoji

    buttons[random_button].update_command(match_emoji, [True])

def match_emoji(matched):
    if matched:
        result.value = "correct"
        score.value = int(score.value) + 1
    else:
        result.value = "incorrect"
        score.value = int(score.value) - 1

    setup_round()

def reduce_time():
    timer.value = int(timer.value) - 1
    # is it game over?
    if int(timer.value) < 0:
        result.value = "Game over! Score = " + score.value
```

emoji4.py (cont.) / Python 3

```python
        # hide the game
        pictures_box.hide()
        buttons_box.hide()
        timer.hide()
        score.hide()


# -------------------------------
# App
# -------------------------------

app = App("emoji match")

score = Text(app, text="0")
timer = Text(app, text="30")

pictures_box = Box(app, layout="grid")
buttons_box = Box(app, layout="grid")

pictures = []
buttons = []

for x in range(0,3):
    for y in range(0,3):
        picture = Picture(pictures_box, grid=[x,y])
        pictures.append(picture)

        button = PushButton(buttons_box, grid=[x,y])
        buttons.append(button)

result = Text(app)

setup_round()

app.repeat(1000, reduce_time)

app.display()
```

09-emoji-match.py / Python 3

```python
# -----------------------------
# Imports
# -----------------------------

import os
from random import shuffle, randint
from guizero import App, Box, Picture,  PushButton, Text


# -----------------------------
# Variables
# -----------------------------

# set the path to the emoji folder on your computer
emojis_dir = "emojis"
emojis = [os.path.join(emojis_dir, f) for f in os.listdir(emojis_dir)]
shuffle(emojis)


# -----------------------------
# Functions
# -----------------------------

def setup_round():
    for picture in pictures:
        picture.image = emojis.pop()

    for button in buttons:
        button.image = emojis.pop()
        button.update_command(match_emoji, args=[False])

    matched_emoji = emojis.pop()

    random_picture = randint(0,8)
    pictures[random_picture].image = matched_emoji

    random_button = randint(0,8)
    buttons[random_button].image = matched_emoji

    buttons[random_button].update_command(match_emoji, [True])
```

09-emoji-match.py (cont.) / Python 3

```python
def match_emoji(matched):
    if matched:
        result.value = "correct"
        score.value = int(score.value) + 1
    else:
        result.value = "incorrect"
        score.value = int(score.value) - 1

    setup_round()

def reduce_time():
    timer.value = int(timer.value) - 1
    # is it game over?
    if int(timer.value) < 0:
        result.value = "Game over! Score = " + score.value
        # hide the game
        game_box.hide()


# ------------------------------
# App
# ------------------------------

app = App("emoji match")

game_box = Box(app, align="top")

top_box = Box(game_box, align="top", width="fill")
Text(top_box, align="left", text="Score ")
score = Text(top_box, text="4", align="left")
timer = Text(top_box, text="30", align="right")
Text(top_box, text="Time", align="right")

pictures_box = Box(game_box, layout="grid")
buttons_box = Box(game_box, layout="grid")

pictures = []
buttons = []

for x in range(0,3):
```

09-emoji-match.py (cont.) / Python 3

```python
    for y in range(0,3):
        picture = Picture(pictures_box, grid=[x,y])
        pictures.append(picture)

        button = PushButton(buttons_box, grid=[x,y])
        buttons.append(button)

result = Text(app)

setup_round()

app.repeat(1000, reduce_time)

app.display()
```

Chapter 10
Paint
Create a simple drawing application

You are going to build a simple application which will allow you to paint using lines and shapes (**Figure 1**). You will create your paint application in four stages:

- drawing dots which follow the mouse
- draw lines between the dots
- adding colours and line width modifier
- drawing shapes

Note that you can style your application anyway you want – it doesn't have to look like this one.

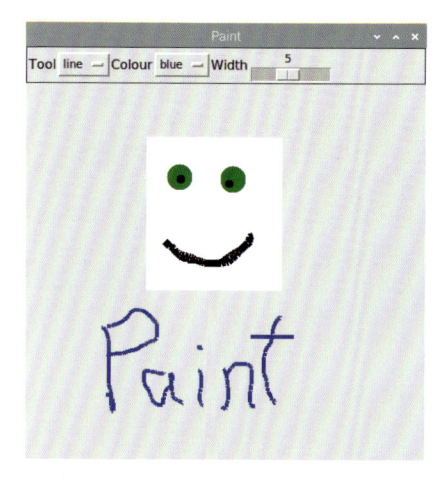

◾ **Figure 1** Our simple paint application

Drawing dots

The first step is to create a simple application which will use the Drawing widget and the `when_mouse_dragged` event to draw dots (or ovals on the screen).

In the imports section of your otherwise blank program, add the widgets:

```
from guizero import App, Drawing
```

Create a new function:

```
def draw(event):
    painting.oval(
        event.x - 1, event.y - 1,
        event.x + 1, event.y + 1,
        color="black")
```

Add this code to the app section:

```
app = App("Paint")

painting = Drawing(app, width="fill", height="fill")

painting.when_mouse_dragged = draw

app.display()
```

Your code should resemble **paint1.py** (page 116). The Drawing widget fills all the available space on the window. When the mouse is dragged across the drawing, the function **draw** is called which draws ovals on the **painting**.

The **draw** function is called each time an event is raised. The event which contains the x and y position of the mouse is passed as a variable to the function.

There is a problem, though. Unless you move your mouse very slowly, a series of dots is drawn by your program, not a continuous line (**Figure 2**). It's not a very good paintbrush! There are gaps between the dots because an event is not raised for every pixel the mouse crosses.

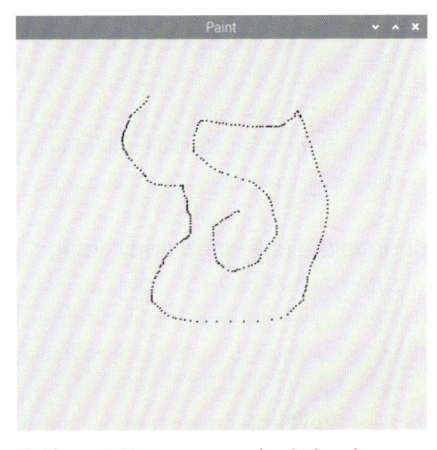

▲ **Figure 2** Not a very good paintbrush

Lines between the dots

To solve this problem, you are going to change the program to draw lines between the dots. That way the line made will be continuous and be more like a pen or paintbrush.

You will need to use a `when_left_button_pressed` event to store the position of where the line starts. Then draw a straight line between where the line starts and next position the mouse was dragged too.

Create a new function which will be called when the mouse is pressed.

```
def start(event):
    painting.last_event = event
```

Add this to the app section:

```
painting.when_left_button_pressed = start
```

The position of where the line starts is stored in the `last_event` variable.

Modify the `draw` function to draw a line between where the line starts and where the mouse has been dragged to.

```
def draw(event):
    painting.line(
        painting.last_event.x, painting.last_event.y,
        event.x, event.y,
        color="black",
        width=3
    )
    painting.last_event = event
```

By updating the `last_event` variable to be the current position of the mouse, the next time the mouse is dragged, it will draw another line between this point and the next. Your program should look like **paint2.py**. Test it and make sure your paintbrush now works properly.

Change the line width and colour

You only have one colour and thickness for your paintbrush, which limits the drawing you can create. Next, you will amend your GUI so you can pick different colours and line widths.

Add two widgets to the GUI capture a colour and width for the line.

```
from guizero import App, Drawing, Combo, Slider
```

Add these line to the app section:

```
color = Combo(app, options=["black", "white", "red", "green", "blue"])
width = Slider(app, start=1, end=10)
```

You may also want to change the background colour of your painting to be different. Also, we have used a Combo and a Slider, but you could choose different widgets.

Modify the **draw** function to use the colour and width values when painting the line.

```
painting.line(
    painting.last_event.x, painting.last_event.y,
    event.x, event.y,
    color=color.value,
    width=width.value
)
```

Test your code, which should be like **paint3.py**, and you can now select the colour and line width.

Drawing shapes

You are going to extend your paint application so you can draw filled rectangles. When the mouse is pressed, the rectangle will appear and grow as the mouse is dragged across the screen. When the mouse button is released, the rectangle will drawn onto the screen.

To do this, you will modify your program to continuously draw and delete rectangles until the mouse button is released. Let's add a widget to your GUI so you can select whether to draw a line or a rectangle. Add this to the app section:

```
shape = Combo(app, options=["line", "rectangle"])
```

Modify the **draw** function to only draw lines if the **"line"** option is selected.

```
if shape.value == "line":
    painting.line(
        painting.last_event.x, painting.last_event.y,
        event.x, event.y,
        color=color.value,
        width=width.value
    )
```

Test your program to make sure that the line still works and nothing happens when **"rectangle"** is selected.

Create two new variables to keep track of the first event and the last shape drawn when the mouse button is pressed.

```
def start(event):
    painting.last_event = event
    painting.first_event = event
    painting.last_shape = None
```

These variables will be used when drawing and deleting the rectangle before the mouse button is released.

Add this code to your draw function to draw a rectangle when the mouse is dragged.

```
if shape.value == "rectangle":

    if painting.last_shape is not None:
        painting.delete(painting.last_shape)

    rectangle = painting.rectangle(
        painting.first_event.x, painting.first_event.y,
        event.x, event.y,
        color=color.value
    )

    painting.last_shape = rectangle
```

The program will continually draw a rectangle, then delete it, then draw it again until you release the button.

Your complete program should look similar to **paint4.py**. Have fun trying it out – what pictures can you create?

> ### ADD OVALS
>
> When you first created the Paint application, you used ovals to draw dots across the screen. Can you modify your program to draw ovals again, using a similar process to how rectangles are drawn? Hint: see the **10-paint.py** listing, which also styles up the tools and aligns them neatly in a box.
>
> The Drawing widget also supports drawing triangles and polygons. Take a look at the documentation (**lawsie.github.io/guizero/drawin**g) and see how you might use this function to create other shapes.

CUSTOM EVENTS

To get your paint application to react to the mouse position, you have used custom events. The events work very similar to the normal widget command parameter in that you set them to a function, which is called when that event occurs.

When your function is called, a variable is passed which contains information about the event that has occurred, such as the x and y co-ordinates of the mouse. Most widgets, including the App itself, support the following events:

- when clicked – `when_clicked`
- when the left mouse button is pressed – `when_left_button_pressed`
- when the left mouse button is released – `when_left_button_released`
- when the right mouse button is pressed – `when_right_button_pressed`
- when the right mouse button is released – `when_right_button_released`
- when a key is pressed – `when_key_pressed`
- when a key is released – `when_key_released`
- when the mouse enters a widget – `when_mouse_enters`
- when the mouse leaves a widget – `when_mouse_leaves`
- when the mouse is dragged across a widget – `when_mouse_dragged`

These events can be used to make your GUIs more interactive.

paint1.py / Python 3

> **DOWNLOAD**
> magpi.cc/guizerocode

```python
# simple paint app, just draw dots

# ------------------------------
# Imports
# ------------------------------

from guizero import App, Drawing



# ------------------------------
# Functions
# ------------------------------

def draw(event):
    painting.oval(
        event.x - 1, event.y - 1,
        event.x + 1, event.y + 1,
        color="black")


# ------------------------------
# App
# ------------------------------

app = App("Paint")

painting = Drawing(app, width="fill", height="fill")

painting.when_mouse_dragged = draw

app.display()
```

paint2.py / Python 3

```python
# drawing lines by tracking when the mouse is clicked

# ------------------------------
# Imports
# ------------------------------

from guizero import App, Drawing


# ------------------------------
# Functions
# ------------------------------

def start(event):
    painting.last_event = event

def draw(event):
    painting.line(
        painting.last_event.x, painting.last_event.y,
        event.x, event.y,
        color="black",
        width=3
    )

    painting.last_event = event


# ------------------------------
# App
# ------------------------------

app = App("Paint")

painting = Drawing(app, width="fill", height="fill")

painting.when_left_button_pressed = start
painting.when_mouse_dragged = draw

app.display()
```

paint3.py / Python 3

```python
# widgets to set the color and width

# -------------------------------
# Imports
# -------------------------------

from guizero import App, Drawing, Combo, Slider


# -------------------------------
# Functions
# -------------------------------

def start(event):
    painting.last_event = event

def draw(event):
    painting.line(
        painting.last_event.x, painting.last_event.y,
        event.x, event.y,
        color=color.value,
        width=width.value
    )


    painting.last_event = event


# -------------------------------
# App
# -------------------------------

app = App("Paint")

color = Combo(app, options=["black", "white", "red", "green", "blue"])
width = Slider(app, start=1, end=10)

painting = Drawing(app, width="fill", height="fill")

painting.when_left_button_pressed = start
painting.when_mouse_dragged = draw

app.display()
```

paint4.py / Python 3

```python
# adding different drawing shapes

# ------------------------------
# Imports
# ------------------------------

from guizero import App, Drawing, Combo, Slider


# ------------------------------
# Functions
# ------------------------------

def start(event):
    painting.last_event = event
    painting.first_event = event
    painting.last_shape = None

def draw(event):
    if shape.value == "line":
        painting.line(
            painting.last_event.x, painting.last_event.y,
            event.x, event.y,
            color=color.value,
            width=width.value
        )

    if shape.value == "rectangle":

        if painting.last_shape is not None:
            painting.delete(painting.last_shape)

        rectangle = painting.rectangle(
            painting.first_event.x, painting.first_event.y,
            event.x, event.y,
            color=color.value
        )

        painting.last_shape = rectangle

    painting.last_event = event


# ------------------------------
# App
```

paint4.py (cont.) / Python 3

```python
# ------------------------------

app = App("Paint")

color = Combo(app, options=["black", "white", "red", "green", "blue"])
width = Slider(app, start=1, end=10)
shape = Combo(app, options=["line", "rectangle"])

painting = Drawing(app, width="fill", height="fill")

painting.when_left_button_pressed = start
painting.when_mouse_dragged = draw

app.display()
```

10-paint.py / Python 3

```python
# styled up

# ------------------------------
# Imports
# ------------------------------

from guizero import App, Drawing, Combo, Slider, Box, Text


# ------------------------------
# Functions
# ------------------------------

def start(event):
    painting.last_event = event
    painting.first_event = event
    painting.last_shape = None

def draw(event):
    if shape.value == "line":
        painting.line(
            painting.last_event.x, painting.last_event.y,
            event.x, event.y,
            color=color.value,
            width=width.value
        )

    else:
        if painting.last_shape is not None:
                painting.delete(painting.last_shape)

        if shape.value == "rectangle":

            painting.last_shape = painting.rectangle(
                painting.first_event.x, painting.first_event.y,
                event.x, event.y,
                color=color.value
            )

        if shape.value == "oval":

            painting.last_shape = painting.oval(
                painting.first_event.x, painting.first_event.y,
                event.x, event.y,
                color=color.value
```

10-paint.py (cont.) / Python 3

```python
        )
    painting.last_event = event


# ------------------------------
# App
# ------------------------------

app = App("Paint")
app.font = "impact"

tools = Box(app, align="top", width="fill", border=True)

Text(tools, text="Tool", align="left")
shape = Combo(tools, options=["line", "rectangle", "oval"],
align="left")

Text(tools, text="Colour", align="left")
color = Combo(tools, options=["black", "white", "red", "green",
"blue"], align="left")

Text(tools, text="Width", align="left")
width = Slider(tools, start=1, end=10, align="left")

painting = Drawing(app, width="fill", height="fill")

painting.when_left_button_pressed = start
painting.when_mouse_dragged = draw

app.display()
```

CREATE GRAPHICAL USER INTERFACES WITH PYTHON

Chapter 10 Paint

Chapter 11
Stop-frame Animation

Build your own stop-frame animated GIF creator

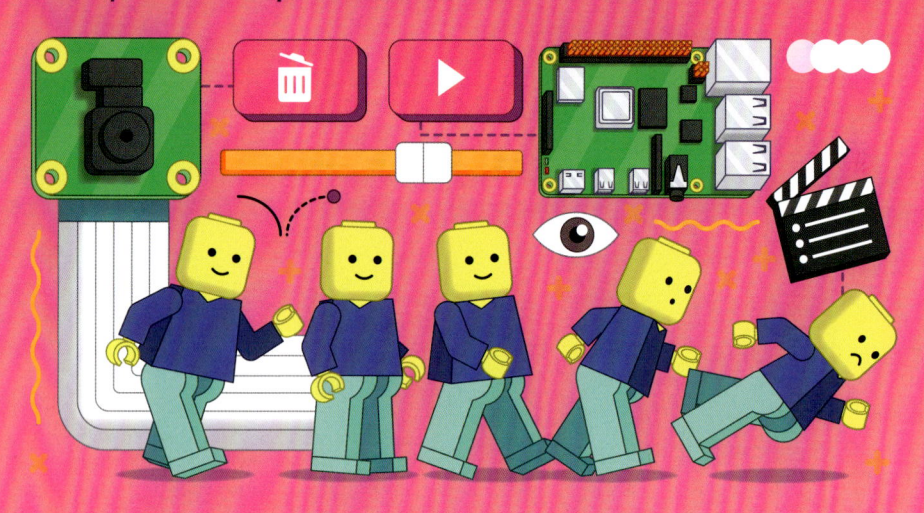

This projects uses a Raspberry Pi Camera Module and guizero to make a stop-frame animation application (**Figure 1**). To complete this project, you will need a Raspberry Pi with an official Camera Module (or High Quality Camera). If you need help connecting up the Camera Module, take a look at the 'Getting started with the Camera Module' guide at **rpf.io/picamera**.

You will need guizero installed with the optional 'images' functionality, which you can install by running this command in the terminal:

```
pip3 install guizero[images]
```

If using the Thonny IDE, you may also need to switch to Regular Mode, go to Tools > Manager packages, select guizero, click on the '...' button, check the box for 'Upgrade dependencies', and click on Install.

CREATE GRAPHICAL USER INTERFACES WITH PYTHON

This project is broken down into stages:

1. Taking a picture with the camera and displaying it on a GUI
2. Taking multiple pictures and saving them to a GIF file
3. Allowing the user to change the GIF
4. Tidying up the GUI

Take a picture

Start by creating this program.

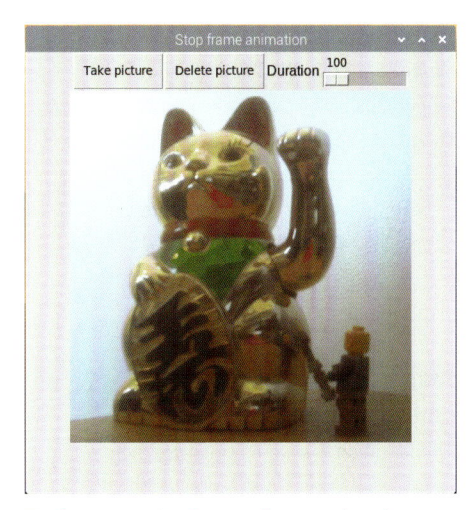

▲ **Figure 1** A simple stop-frame animation

```python
# Imports ---------------
from guizero import App, Picture, PushButton
from picamera import PiCamera

# Functions -------------
def capture_image():
    camera.capture("frame.jpg")
    viewer.image = "frame.jpg"

# Variables -------------
camera = PiCamera(resolution="400x400")

# App -------------------
app = App(title="Stop frame animation")

take_next_picture = PushButton(app, text="Take picture",
 command=capture_image)
viewer = Picture(app)

app.display()
```

Note that the higher the resolution, the greater the processing time. 400×400 is small but really quick to process.

The GUI contains a PushButton and Picture. When the button is pressed, the `capture_image` function is called. The function uses the camera to capture an image and save it as **frame.jpg**. The picture is then displayed in the Picture widget.

Test the program (**stopframe1.py**, page 131). When you click the 'Take picture' button, the image should be displayed on the GUI (**Figure 2**).

Take multiple images and save to a GIF

An animation is made of multiple pictures, known as frames. Each frame in the animation will be slightly different to the last and when played together at speed, the animation will appear to move.

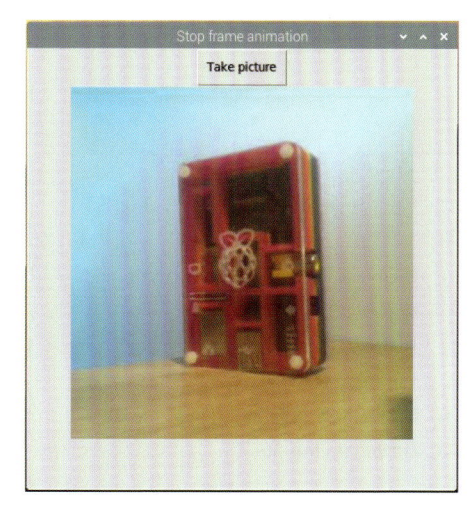

🔺 **Figure 2** Take a picture

In this step, you will change your GUI to keep a list of all the frames taken and use PIL (Python Imaging Library) to save the frames as an animated GIF which will be displayed in the viewer. At the top of your program, import the Image module from PIL:

```
from PIL import Image
```

Create a list to store the frames of your animation:

```
frames = []
```

To keep track of how many frames have been taken, import a Text widget, add it to your app, and set it to 0.

```
from guizero import App, Picture, PushButton, Text

total_frames = Text(app, text="0")
```

Each time a new image is captured, you will need to open it and append it to your list of frames:

```
def capture_image():
    camera.capture("frame.jpg")
    viewer.image = "frame.jpg"

    frame = Image.open("frame.jpg")
    frames.append(frame)
    total_frames.value = len(frames)
```

The `len` (length) of the `frames` list is then used to update the text in `total_frames`.

Your program should now look similar to **stopframe2.py**. Test it and make sure the number of frames increases each time you take a picture.

Save as a GIF

You can PIL to save all the frames as one animated GIF. Create a new `save_animation` function to save the frames as **animation.gif**.

```
def save_animation():
    if len(frames) > 0:
        viewer.show()
        frames[0].save(
            "animation.gif",
            save_all=True,
            append_images=frames[1:])
        viewer.image = "animation.gif"
    else:
        viewer.hide()
```

There is a lot happening here, but by breaking down the code you can see how this works.

If the number of frames in the list is greater than 0, then the viewer is shown, otherwise it is hidden:

```
if len(frames) > 0:
    viewer.show()
    ...
else:
    viewer.hide()
```

The frames are then saved to a file called **animation.gif**. The first frame (`frames[0]`) is saved, the remaining frames (`frames[1:]`) are appended, and all are saved to the animated GIF:

```
frames[0].save(
    "animation.gif",
    save_all=True,
    append_images=frames[1:])
```

The **animation.gif** is then shown in the viewer:

```
viewer.image = "animation.gif"
```

Call the **save_animation** function at the *end* of the **capture_image** function to create and display the animation:

```
def capture_image():
    camera.capture("frame.jpg")
    viewer.image = "frame.jpg"

    save_animation()
```

Your code should now be similar to **stopframe3.py**. Test it out.

Delete the last frame

At the moment, if you make a mistake while creating your animated GIF, you have to start again from the beginning.

You should modify your GUI to allow the last frame taken to be deleted, so if a mistake is made you can undo the change.

Create a new function which will remove or pop the last frame from the list, save the changed animation, and then display it.

```
def delete_frame():
    if len(frames) > 0:
        frames.pop()
        total_frames.value = len(frames)

    save_animation()
```

The length of the **frames** list is checked before attempting to pop the last item. An error would be raised if you tried to pop an item from an empty list.

Add a PushButton to the GUI to call the **delete_frame** function, by inserting this code in your app:

```
delete_last_picture = PushButton(controls, align="left",
text="Delete last", command=delete_frame)
```

Note: *You could also modify the GUI to allow you to delete any frame, not just the last one.*

Changing the timing

Each frame is displayed for the default duration time of 100 milliseconds. Include a Slider widget in your GUI to allow the duration to be changed.

Add it to the list of imports.

```
from guizero import App, Picture, PushButton, Text, Slider
```

Then create the widget in the app.

```
Text(app, text="Duration")
duration = Slider(app, start=100, end=1000, command=save_animation)
```

The **start** and **end** parameters will be the minimum and maximum times you can set for the frame duration.

Each time the slider is changed, the **save_animation** function will be run.

Update the **save_animation** function to use the duration value when saving the GIF.

```
    frames[0].save(
        "animation.gif",
        save_all=True,
        append_images=frames[1:],
        duration=duration.value)
```

Your code should now resemble **stopframe4.py**. Try it out.

> ### CONSISTENT CAPTURES
>
> As the camera is using **"auto"**, each time a image is captured, the setting used may change. This will cause each image to be slightly different and will cause a flickering in your animation.
>
> By fixing the camera settings when the program starts, you can stop this from happening.
>
> The required settings will depend on the lighting where you are taking picture.
>
> This article from the picamera documentation provides more information and example settings: **rpf.io/picamera-consistent**.

Align the controls

At the moment, the controls are taking up a lot of room stacked at the top of the GUI (**Figure 3**). Create a Box and align it to the top of the GUI to hold the controls, first adding it to the imports.

```
from guizero import App, Picture, PushButton, Text, Slider, Box

controls = Box(app, align="top")
```

Modify the widgets so that they are in the controls box and set the align parameter to **"left"**. For example:

```
total_frames = Text(controls, text="0", align="left")
```

Aligning widgets to the left inside the box will make them stack up next to each other.

Repeat this for rest of the controls so they are all put into the top box and lined up next to each other.

Your complete program should look similar to **11-stop-frame.py**.

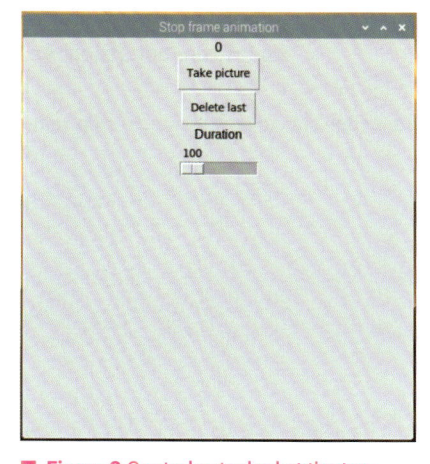

🔺 **Figure 3** Controls stacked at the top

stopframe1.py / Python 3

```python
# Imports ---------------

from guizero import App, Picture, PushButton
from picamera import PiCamera


# Functions -------------

def capture_image():
    camera.capture("frame.jpg")
    viewer.image = "frame.jpg"


# App -------------------

app = App(title="Stop frame animation")

camera = PiCamera(resolution="400x400")
take_next_picture = PushButton(app, text="Take picture", command=capture_image)
viewer = Picture(app)

app.display()
```

DOWNLOAD
magpi.cc/guizerocode

stopframe2.py / Python 3

```python
# Imports ---------------

from guizero import App, Picture, PushButton, Text
from picamera import PiCamera
from PIL import Image


# Functions -------------

def capture_image():
    camera.capture("frame.jpg")
    viewer.image = "frame.jpg"
```

stopframe2.py (cont.) / Python 3

```python
    frame = Image.open("frame.jpg")
    frames.append(frame)
    total_frames.value = len(frames)


# Variables --------------

frames = []

camera = PiCamera(resolution="400x400")


# App -------------------

app = App(title="Stop frame animation")

total_frames = Text(app, text="0")
take_next_picture = PushButton(app, text="Take picture", command=capture_image)

viewer = Picture(app)

app.display()
```

stopframe3.py / Python 3

```python
# Imports ---------------

from guizero import App, Picture, PushButton, Text
from picamera import PiCamera
from PIL import Image


# Functions -------------

def capture_image():
    camera.capture("frame.jpg")
    viewer.image = "frame.jpg"

    frame = Image.open("frame.jpg")
```

stopframe3.py (cont.) / Python 3

```python
    frames.append(frame)
    total_frames.value = len(frames)
    
    save_animation()

def save_animation():
    if len(frames) > 0:
        viewer.show()
        frames[0].save(
            "animation.gif",
            save_all=True,
            append_images=frames[1:])
        viewer.image = "animation.gif"
    else:
        viewer.hide()


# Variables --------------

frames = []

camera = PiCamera(resolution="400x400")


# App --------------------

app = App(title="Stop frame animation")

total_frames = Text(app, text="0")
take_next_picture = PushButton(app, text="Take picture",
command=capture_image)

viewer = Picture(app)

app.display()
```

stopframe4.py / Python 3

```python
# Imports ---------------

from guizero import App, Picture, PushButton, Text, Slider
from picamera import PiCamera
from PIL import Image


# Functions -------------

def capture_image():
    camera.capture("frame.jpg")
    viewer.image = "frame.jpg"

    frame = Image.open("frame.jpg")
    frames.append(frame)
    total_frames.value = len(frames)

    save_animation()

def save_animation():
    if len(frames) > 0:
        viewer.show()
        frames[0].save(
            "animation.gif",
            save_all=True,
            append_images=frames[1:],
            duration=duration.value)
        viewer.image = "animation.gif"
    else:
        viewer.hide()

def delete_frame():
    if len(frames) > 0:
        frames.pop()
        total_frames.value = len(frames)

    save_animation()


# Variables -------------

frames = []

camera = PiCamera(resolution="400x400")
```

stopframe4.py (cont.) / Python 3

```python
# App ------------------

app = App(title="Stop frame animation")

total_frames = Text(app, text="0")
take_next_picture = PushButton(app, text="Take picture",
command=capture_image)
delete_last_picture = PushButton(app, text="Delete last",
command=delete_frame)
Text(app, text="Duration")
duration = Slider(app, start=100, end=1000, command=save_
animation)

viewer = Picture(app)

app.display()
```

11-stop-frame.py / Python 3

```python
# Imports ---------------

from guizero import App, Picture, PushButton, Text, Slider, Box
from picamera import PiCamera
from PIL import Image


# Functions -------------

def capture_image():
    camera.capture("frame.jpg")
    viewer.image = "frame.jpg"
    
    frame = Image.open("frame.jpg")
    frames.append(frame)
    total_frames.value = len(frames)
    
    save_animation()

def save_animation():
    if len(frames) > 0:
        viewer.show()
        frames[0].save(
```

11-stop-frame.py (cont.) / Python 3

```python
            "animation.gif",
            save_all=True,
            append_images=frames[1:],
            duration=duration.value)
        viewer.image = "animation.gif"
    else:
        viewer.hide()

def delete_frame():
    if len(frames) > 0:
        frames.pop()
        total_frames.value = len(frames)

    save_animation()


# Variables -------------

frames = []

camera = PiCamera(resolution="400x400")


# App -------------------

app = App(title="Stop frame animation")

controls = Box(app, align="top")
total_frames = Text(controls, text="0", align="left")
take_next_picture = PushButton(controls, align="left", text="Take picture", command=capture_image)
delete_last_picture = PushButton(controls, align="left", text="Delete last", command=delete_frame)
Text(controls, align="left", text="Duration")
duration = Slider(controls, align="left", start=100, end=1000, command=save_animation)

viewer = Picture(app)

app.display()
```

CREATE GRAPHICAL USER INTERFACES WITH PYTHON

Appendix A
Setting up
Learn how install Python and an IDE

Here we will show you how to set everything up on your computer in order to create Python programs with graphical user interfaces. To be able to run and edit the applications in this book, you'll need three things:

1. The Python interpreter – this is the software that allows you to run programs written in Python.
2. An integrated development environment (IDE) – software which includes a code editor and the ability to run a program from that editor. Python comes bundled with an IDE called IDLE, but you might choose to use a different IDE.
3. The guizero Python library – instructions for installing this are given in Chapter 1, but if you are using Thonny please refer to the section below as the instructions are slightly different.

There are many IDEs available; here we're going to look at two of them – IDLE and Thonny. IDLE is a very simple IDE which comes bundled with Python for Windows and Mac, and is installed by default on some versions of Raspberry Pi OS. Thonny has some additional features, but it is still geared towards beginners.

Occasionally, errors can occur while trying to get everything installed and running – especially on older computers. If you experience errors while trying to use a particular IDE or version of Python, try another IDE or Python version.

CREATE GRAPHICAL USER INTERFACES WITH PYTHON

Installing Python and IDLE

Windows

Windows does not come with Python 3 pre-installed. If you think you may have installed Python previously, you can check this by looking for 'Python' in the Start menu or under 'Apps and Features' within Settings. If you intend to use Thonny as your IDE, you can skip ahead to the 'Thonny' section as Python is automatically installed alongside it.

Go to **python.org**, mouse-over Downloads and click on Windows. Choose the option to directly download the latest stable Python 3 release (most people will need the one labelled *Windows x86-64 executable installer*, but this may vary depending on your computer). Once the download is complete, run the program either via your web browser or from your Downloads folder. Click 'Install now' to install using the default options. IDLE will also be installed and can be opened via the Start menu or by searching for it by name.

Alternatively, if you have Windows 10, you could download the Microsoft Store package of the latest Python version (currently 3.8). If you have any difficulties, full installation instructions can be found at **rpf.io/python-windows**.

Mac

Although most versions of macOS come with a Python interpreter, it's version 2.7 which is not compatible with guizero. You will need to install Python 3 alongside the existing installation.

Go to **python.org**, mouse-over Downloads and click on Mac OS X. Choose the latest stable release, and click on *macOS 64-bit installer*. Once the download is complete, run the program either via your web browser or from your Downloads folder. Install using the default options. IDLE will also be installed and can now be opened from the Launchpad or Applications folder.

Raspberry Pi

Raspberry Pi OS (previously known as Raspbian) comes with Python already installed. However, recent versions of the OS come with the Thonny but do not include IDLE. To install IDLE, make sure you are connected to the internet, then open a Terminal and type:

```
sudo apt-get install idle3
```

If you have any problems getting the code in this book to run, try upgrading to the most recent version of Raspberry Pi OS.

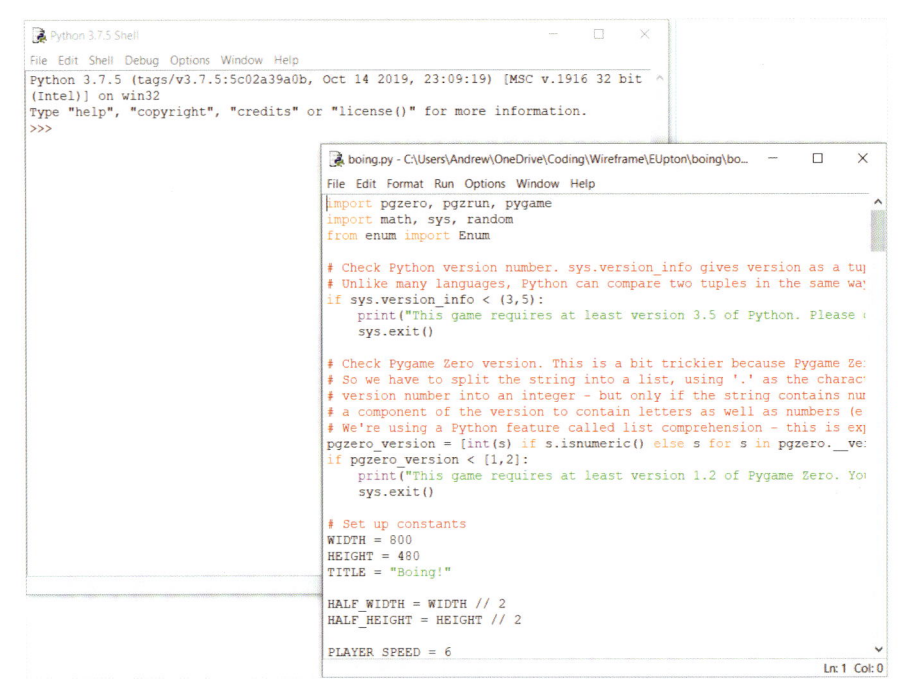

▲ IDLE usually comes pre-installed with Python

IDEs

IDLE

IDLE is a basic IDE which is usually automatically installed alongside Python. Once IDLE starts, the first thing you'll see is a window titled 'Python 3.8.5 Shell' (the number may be different depending on which exact version you have). This window is called the *shell* and you can use it to type a line of Python code and see the code run straight away.

For example, try typing the following:

6 + 2

Use the File menu > New file to open a Python file. A file allows you to type multiple lines of code and then run them all, rather than each line running immediately when you press **ENTER**. You can run the program by going to the Run menu and choosing Run Module – or by pressing **F5** on the keyboard. If an error occurs, you will see any error messages in the shell window.

CREATE GRAPHICAL USER INTERFACES WITH PYTHON

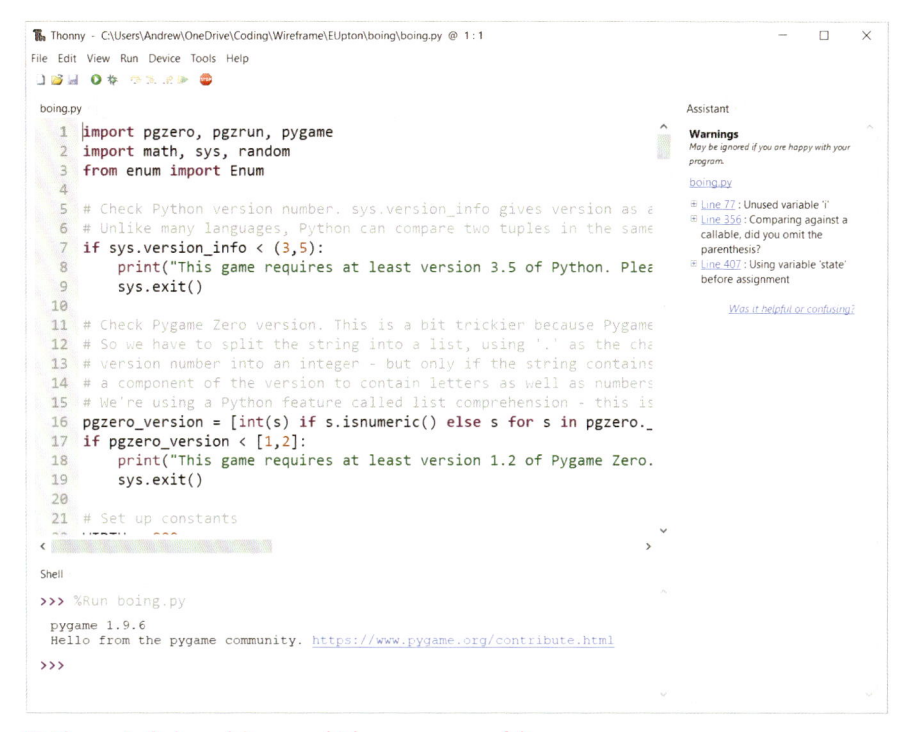

△ Thonny includes a debugger which may prove useful

Thonny

Thonny comes installed with recent versions of Raspberry Pi OS. For Windows and Mac computers, you can download and install it from **thonny.org**. By default, Thonny uses a version of Python which comes packaged with it, so even if you have already installed Python, Thonny will ignore that version and use its own.

Use the File menu > New to open a Python file. You will type your code in the top white box which has a number 1 to the left side. You can run the program by selecting the 'Run current script' button, or by pressing **F5** on the keyboard. If an error occurs, you will see any error messages in the shell area at the bottom of the screen.

Thonny includes a debugger which allows you to step through the code one line at a time and see how the variables change.

Because Thonny uses its own Python installation, you will need to install guizero from inside Thonny in order for Thonny to be able to access it. Make sure you are connected to the internet, then click on the Tools menu > Manage packages. In the window that appears, type guizero in the box and click 'Find package from PyPI'. Thonny will locate the package for you; click Install to install guizero within Thonny's own Python environment.

Appendix B
Get started with Python

If you're a complete beginner, here's how to start coding in Python

Unlike a visual, block-based coding environment like Scratch, **Python is text-based: you write instructions, using a simplified language and specific format, which the computer then carries out.** Python is a great next step for those who have already used Scratch, offering increased flexibility and a more 'traditional' programming environment. In the following examples, we're using the Thonny IDE (integrated development environment), but you can use an alternative IDE if you prefer (see **Appendix A**).

First program
The top white box in the Thonny window is where you write your program script. Click in this box and type the following code:

```
print ("Hello, World!")
```

Now click the Run icon in the Thonny toolbar and you will be asked to save your program first; type a descriptive name, like 'Hello World', and click the Save button. Once your program has saved, you'll see two messages appear in the Python shell area:

```
>>> %Run 'Hello World.py'
Hello, World!
```

Congratulations, you have successfully written and run a Python script! You will use the same method for all of the programs in this book – write the code in the script area and then run it.

Loops and code indentation

Just as Scratch uses stacks of jigsaw-like blocks to control which bits of the program are connected to which other bits, Python has its own way of controlling the sequence in which its programs run: indentation.

Create a new program by clicking on the New icon in the Thonny toolbar. You won't lose your existing program; instead, Thonny will create a new tab above the script area. Type in the following code:

```python
print ("Loop starting!")
for i in range(10):
    print ("Loop")
```

Click the Run icon in the Thonny toolbar, save your program with the name 'Indentation', and watch the shell area for its output. See if you can work out what is happening.

The first line prints a message to the shell, just like your Hello World program. The second tells Python to start a loop which runs 10 times – the number of times the loop runs is controlled by the `range(10)` instruction. The third line is indented, which means it is pushed inwards compared to the other lines. This indentation is how Python tells the difference between instructions outside the loop and instructions inside the loop. In Scratch, the instructions to be included in the loop are placed within the C-shaped block, and in Python they are indented. So this means that the instruction to print the word 'Loop' is repeated 10 times.

You'll notice that when you pressed **ENTER** at the end of the third line, Thonny automatically indented the next line, assuming it would be part of the loop. To remove this, just press the **BACKSPACE** key once and then type a fourth and final line:

```python
print ("Loop finished!")
```

Your four-line program is now complete. The first line sits outside the loop, and will only run once; the second line sets up the loop; the third sits inside the loop and will run once for each time the loop loops; and the fourth line sits outside the loop once again.

Run the program again. If you haven't made the Thonny window larger, you may need to use the scroll bar to the right of the shell area to see its full output:

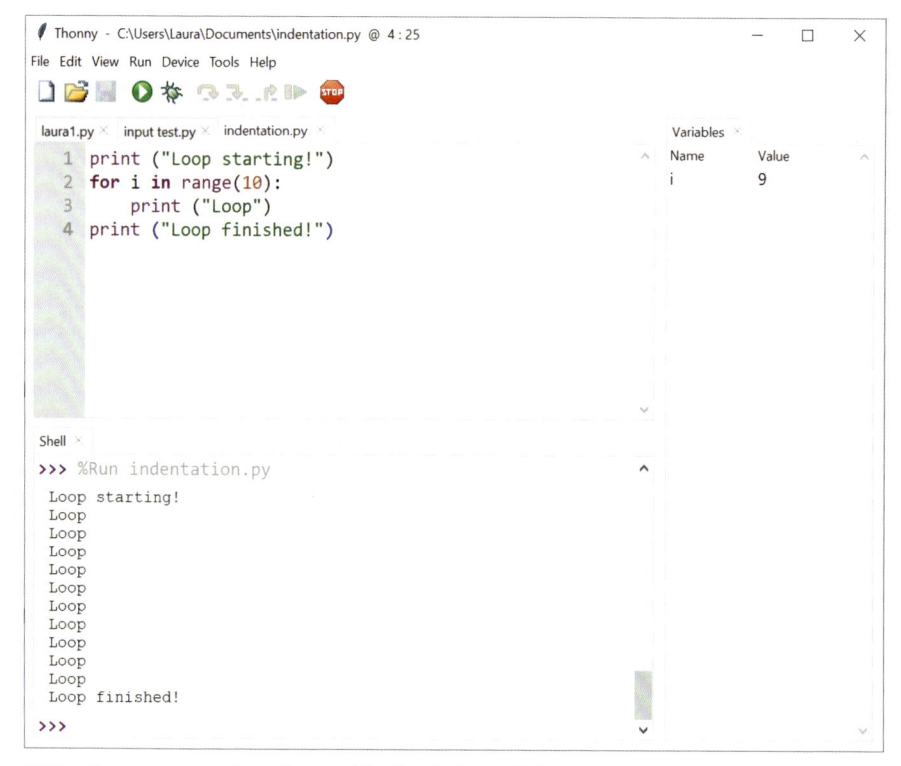

```
Loop starting!
Loop
Loop
Loop
Loop
Loop
Loop
Loop
Loop
Loop
Loop
Loop finished!
```

▲ Run the program and see the result in the shell area below

CREATE GRAPHICAL USER INTERFACES WITH PYTHON

Indentation is a powerful part of Python, and one of the most common reasons for a program to not work as you expected. When looking for problems in a program, always double-check the indentation.

Conditionals and Variables

You can create variables in your program to store values; for example, you might want to store some data the user typed in, or the result of a calculation.

Start a new program by clicking the New icon on the Thonny menu, then type the following into the script area:

```python
my_name = input("What is your name? ")
```

Click the Run icon, save your program with the name 'Input test', and watch what happens in the shell area: you'll be asked for your name. Type your name and press **ENTER**. The variables area to the right of the Thonny window will automatically display the name of the variable

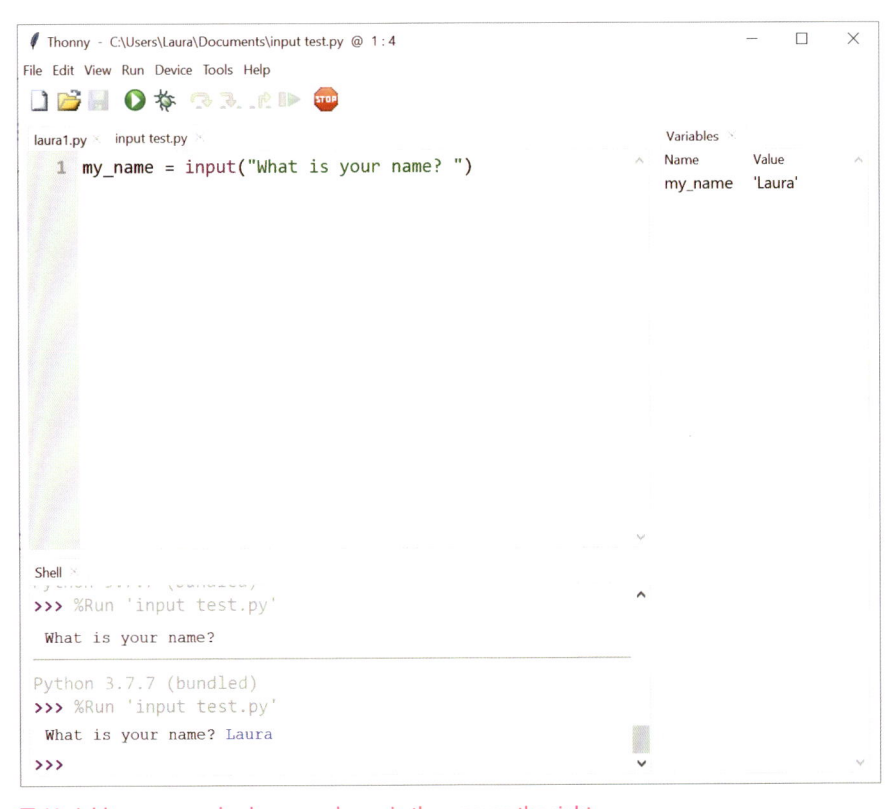

▲ Variable names and values are shown in the area on the right

Appendix B Get started with Python   145

(my_name) and its value (e.g. 'Laura'). If you can't see the variables area, check on the View menu that there is a tick next to Variables. This information remains displayed even when the program isn't running, making it easy to see what your program has been doing.

The program has saved what you typed as your name as the value of the variable called **my_name**. Using the `input` command is useful for basic Python programs, but when you attempt the GUI programs in this book, you will learn about other ways to capture input from the user and store it in variables to be used in your program.

To make your program do something useful with the name, add a conditional statement by typing the following:

```python
if my_name == "Clark Kent":
    print ("You are Superman!")
else:
    print ("You are not Superman!")
```

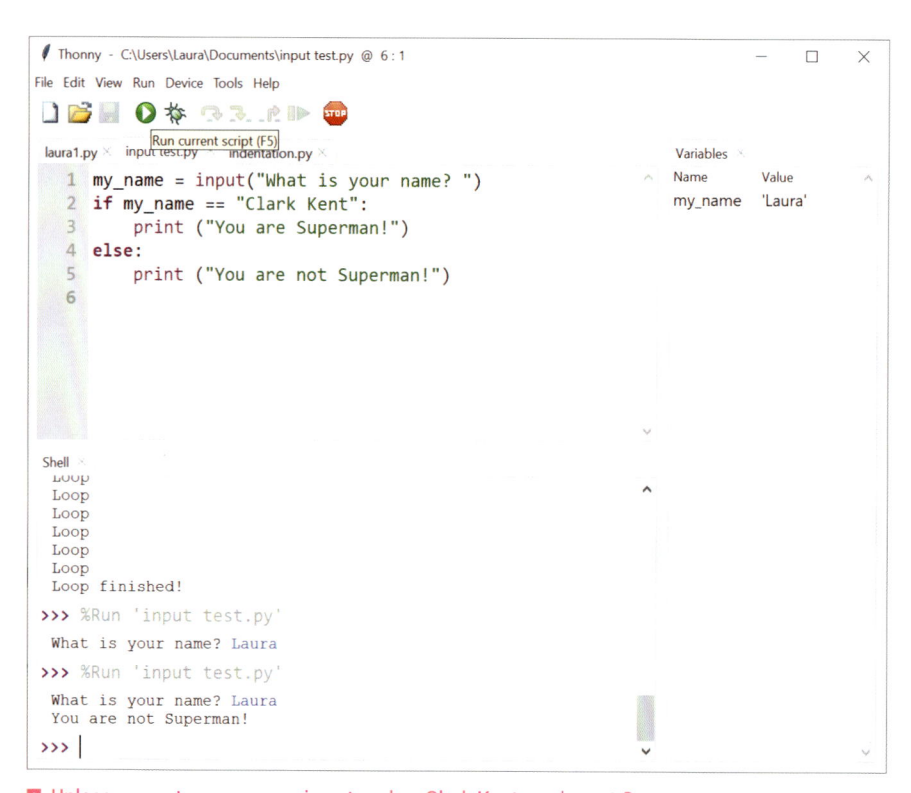

⚠ Unless you enter your name is entered as Clark Kent, you're not Superman

Remember that when Thonny sees that your code needs to be indented, it will do so automatically – but it doesn't know when your code needs to stop being indented, so you'll have to delete the spaces yourself.

Click the Run icon and type your name into the shell area, as before. Unless your name happens to be Clark Kent, you'll see an additional message 'You are not Superman!' in the shell area. Click Run again, and this time type in the name 'Clark Kent' – making sure to write it exactly as in the program, with a capital C and a capital K. This time, the program recognises that you are, in fact, Superman.

The `==` symbol tells Python to compare two values. In this case it will look to see if the value of the variable `my_name` matches the text `"Clark Kent"`.

> ### USING = AND ==
> We have now seen two different operators – the single equals sign (=) and the double equals sign (==). They mean different things and it is important to know the difference. The single equals (=) means "it IS equal to this value," while a double equals (==) means "IS IT equal to this value?" The first is used to assign a value to a variable, and the second is used to compare two values.

When you are creating the programs in this book, you will collect input from the user, store data in variables, display information on the screen, and use loops. The examples we have worked through in this section are very basic and only allow the user to interact with the program via text. We hope that now you know the basics of how to write a Python program you will enjoy creating GUIs as a more graphical way of interacting with your program.

Appendix C
Widgets in guizero

An overview of the widgets used in guizero

Widgets in guizero are how you create your graphical user interface. They are the things which appear on the GUI, everything from the app itself to text boxes, buttons and pictures.

Note: *This is an overview of the widgets in guizero. Be sure to view the specific online documentation for each widget for more information:* **lawsie.github.io/guizero**.

Widgets

App
The App object is the basis of all GUIs created using guizero. It is the main window which contains all of the other widgets.

```
app = App()
app.display()
```

Box
The Box object is an invisible container which can contain other widgets.

```
box = Box(app)
box = Box(app, border=True)
```

ButtonGroup

The ButtonGroup object displays a group of radio buttons, allowing the user to choose a single option.

```
choice = ButtonGroup(app,
 options=["cheese", "ham", "salad"])
```

CheckBox

The CheckBox object displays a check box to allow an option to be ticked or un-ticked.

```
checkbox = CheckBox(app, text="salad ?")
```

Combo

The Combo object displays a drop-down box allowing a single item to be selected from a list of options.

```
combo = Combo(app, options=["cheese",
 "ham", "salad"])
```

Drawing

The Drawing object allows shapes, images, and text to be created.

```
drawing = Drawing(app)
```

ListBox

The ListBox object displays a list of items from which either single or multiple items can be selected.

```
listbox = ListBox(app, items=["cheese",
 "ham", "salad"])
```

Picture
The Picture object displays an image.

```
picture = Picture(app, image="guizero.png")
```

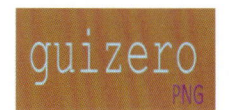

PushButton
The PushButton object displays a button with text or an image, which calls a function when pressed.

```
def do_nothing():
    print("button pressed")

button = PushButton(app, command=do_nothing)
```

Slider
The Slider object displays a bar and selector which can be used to specify a value in a range.

```
slider = Slider(app)
```

Text
The Text object displays non-editable text in your app – useful for titles, labels, and instructions.

```
text = Text(app, text="Hello World")
```

TextBox
The TextBox object displays a text box which the user can type in.

```
textbox = TextBox(app)
```

Waffle

The Waffle object displays an n×n grid of squares with custom dimensions and padding.

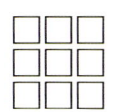

```
waffle = Waffle(app)
```

Window

The Window object creates a new window in guizero.

```
window = Window(app)
```

Properties

All widgets are customisable through their properties. These properties are typical for most widgets. Check a widget's online documentation (e.g. **lawsie.github.io/guizero/app**) for details.

PROPERTY	DATA TYPE	DESCRIPTION
align	string	The alignment of this widget within its container
bg	string, List	The background colour of the widget
enabled	boolean	True if the widget is enabled
font	string	The font of the text
grid	List	[x,y] co-ordinates of this widget if in a 'grid'
height	int, string	The height of the widget
master	App, Window, Box	The container to which this widget belongs
value	int, string, bool	The widget's current 'value', e.g. the text in a TextBox
visible	boolean	If this widget is visible
width	size	The width of the widget
ext_size	int	The size of the text
ext_color	color	The colour of the text

Methods

Widgets can be interacted with through their methods. The methods supported are dependent on the widget, so check the documentation. These methods are typical across most widgets.

METHOD	DESCRIPTION
`after(time, command, args=None)`	Schedules a single call to command after time milliseconds
`cancel(command)`	Cancels a scheduled call to command
`destroy()`	Destroys the widget
`disable()`	Disables the widget so that it cannot be interacted with
`enable()`	Enables the widget
`focus()`	Gives focus to the widget
`hide()`	Hides the widget from view
`repeat(time, command, args=None)`	Schedules a call to command every time milliseconds
`resize(width, height)`	Sets the width and height of the widget
`show()`	Displays the widget if it was previously hidden
`update_command(command, args=None)`	Updates the function to call when the widget is used